JIM'S JOURNEY

THROUGH THE BIBLE
— BOOK I —

By Jim Binns
Edited by Gary Ray

Disclaimer: Copyright © 2025 by Jim Binns. All rights reserved. You may quote and use up to 3,000 words for non-commercial personal use without prior permission from Covenant Press. Commercial use requires proper bibliographic attribution and is limited to 1,000 words without prior permission. Any use beyond these limitations must be approved by Covenant Press.

Covenant Press — New York, New York — ISBN: 978-1-954419-25-4

The journey of a thousand miles begins with a single step.

—𝔍𝔦𝔪 𝔅𝔦𝔫𝔫𝔰

Introduction

The journey of a thousand miles begins with a single step . . .

    I started this journey with the intention of putting together a basic flowchart that would help me understand biblical events that would be taking place beginning at the Rapture until the New Heaven and New Earth are created. The project became more complex as I searched scriptures, related documents composed by evangelical leaders, discussions with bible scholars, and many other internet sources. Understanding specifics about certain bible verses often requires understanding many other associated verses. I have read that the first draft of what you do is just to tell yourself the story.

    To that end, I have tried to put together a flow of events that would capture the essence of what prophecy states will take place from the Rapture until Jesus returns for His Church and this world is made anew.

    I never intended to put together "a book," but as the scriptures unfolded, so did the number of pages in my document. As you read through the topics listed, I hope they will give you a better understanding of the path leading us to an eternity with the King of Kings and Lord of Lords.

    First, I do not sit down at my desk to put something already clear in my mind into verse. If it were clear in my mind, I should have no incentive or need to write about it. *"We do not write in order to be understood; we write in order to understand."* C. S. Lewis

    Eschatology (es-cha-tol-a-ge) is a branch of Christian doctrine concerning the study of end times. However, interpreting the book of Revelation is a challenging area of Christian doctrine. There has been a wide diversity of thought among Christians concerning the study of last things, such as

Christ's future return, the Rapture, the Resurrection, Final Judgments, and the New Heaven and New Earth.

In most other religions, heaven is gained based on the amount of works you do in your life. In other words, you must work to earn it. Christianity is the only religion where works do not obtain heaven, but by what was done for you. Heaven is not the reward for your good works; it is the reward for your <u>faith</u>.

"For <u>God so loved the world</u> that he gave his one and only Son, that whoever believes in him shall not perish but have eternal life" (John 3:16).

Jesus' resurrection from the dead and the empty tomb prove that He lives, and so shall we.

I love the statement in one of Tim LaHaye's books: *"Prophecy is history written in advance."* I know that only God can predict the future with perfect accuracy, but I also believe that the worst days in history are not behind us but are still ahead of us.

"My heart overflows with a good theme; I address my verses to the King; My tongue is the pen of a ready writer" (Psalms 45:1).

"All scripture is inspired by God and is useful for teaching, for reproof, for correction, and for training in righteousness, so that everyone who belongs to God may be proficient, equipped for every good work."

—*Paul the Apostle* (2 Timothy 3:16–17)

Table of Contents

PART I: THE BEGINNING OF THE JOURNEY **5**

    HEAVEN 5
    GOD 6
    JESUS 6
    THE HOLY SPIRIT 7
    THE HOLY TRINITY 8
    THE BIBLE 8
    THE DEVIL 8
    THE ANTICHRIST (BEAST) 9
    THE FALSE PROPHET 9
    MARK OF THE BEAST 9
    THE UNHOLY TRINITY 10
    HELL 10
    THE RAPTURE 11
    MARRIAGE SUPPER OF THE LAMB 13
    JUDGMENT SEAT OF CHRIST (THE BEMA) 13
    THE TRIBULATION 15
    TWO WITNESSES 16
    THE 144,000 17
    THE "SILENT WITNESS" 17
    AN ANGEL SENT BY GOD 17
    THE TRIBULATION SAINTS 17
    BATTLE OF ARMAGEDDON 18
    THE TRIBULATION ENDS 19
    THE MILLENNIUM BEGINS 20
    MILLENNIUM ENDS 21
    THE GREAT WHITE THRONE JUDGMENT 21
    THE KINGDOM 22
    HOLY CITY: NEW JERUSALEM 24
    ETERNITY BEGINS 26

PART II: THOSE FASCINATING THINGS IN THE BIBLE **27**

    UNICORNS 27
    LEVIATHAN, THE SEA MONSTER 29
    THE NEPHILIM 30
    BEHEMOTH 32
    COCKATRICE 33
    DRAGONS 34

PART III: MISCELLANEOUS TOPICS 36

BODY, SPIRIT, SOUL & HOLY SPIRIT REVISITED 36
THE GIFT OF GROWING OLD 42
WILL I SEE MY BABY IN HEAVEN? 49
COMING HOME 55
THE SEVEN SPIRITS OF GOD 57
WHAT DOES THE NUMBER 40 MEAN IN THE BIBLE? 60
GOD BALANCES THE UNIVERSE 63
COVENANTS IN THE BIBLE 69
THE SCROLL WITH SEVEN SEALS IN REVELATION 81
CHRISTIANITY AND JUDAISM 86
DO HUMAN BEINGS TRULY HAVE FREE WILL? 101
PREDESTINATION VS. FREE WILL? 104
CALENDARS THROUGHOUT THE WORLD 107
DISPENSATIONS 118
GOD AND TIME 126
JESUS FAMILY AND THE APOSTLES 131
WHO OWNS THE LAND? 148

CREDITS **157**

Part I: The Beginning of the Journey

Heaven

Mentioned about 700 times in the Bible. The Lord looks down from heaven and sees all mankind (Psalms 33:13).

"Men of Galilee," they said, "why do you stand here looking into the sky? This same Jesus, who has been taken from you into heaven, will come back in the same way you have seen him go into heaven" (Acts 1:11).

Jesus revealed that heaven is real and that God the Father dwells there. It's a place created by God. A place reserved for us who believe. The Bible mentions three heavens. Paul the Apostle writes:

"I know a person in Christ who fourteen years ago was caught up to the third heaven—whether in the body or out of the body I do not know; God knows" (2 Corinthians).

The first heaven is the immediate atmosphere with the sky and clouds. The second heaven is the vast universe where the sun, moon, stars, and galaxies abide. The third heaven is where the very throne of God resides and where Jesus presently sits at the Lord's right hand.

"In My Father's house are many mansions; if it were not so, I would have told you. I go to prepare a place for you. And if I go and prepare a place for you, I will come again and receive you to Myself; that where I am, there you may be also" (John 14:2–3).

God

Biblical Orthodox Christianity teaches that God the Father is the eternal and supreme being who created and preserves everything. **The Bible is the Word of God** and is a primary source of insight about God's essence and authority.

In the beginning, God created the heavens and the earth. Every good and perfect gift is from above, coming down from the Father of the heavenly lights, who does not change like shifting shadows. God is unique, sovereign, and unchanging. God is omnipotent—all-powerful. He is omnipresent—present everywhere. He is omnibenevolent—all-loving. And He is omniscient—all-knowing.

God is infinite, eternal, unchangeable in his being, wisdom, power, holiness, justice, goodness, and truth. Key names for God are—God the High and Exalted One, Yahweh (The Lord), "I Am," and Father (Abba). <u>God the Father is the First person of the Trinity</u>.

Jesus

Also referred to as Jesus of Nazareth, Jesus Christ (Anointed One), or **Immanuel** (God is with us). He is the incarnation of God the Son and the awaited messiah (the Christ), prophesied in the Hebrew bible. <u>He is the Second person of the Trinity</u>. Jesus was a Galilean Jew, often called "rabbi" and "teacher." He was crucified as a sacrifice to achieve atonement for sin, rose from the dead, and ascended into Heaven, where he sits at the right hand of God (John 16:23).

The first coming of Jesus provided salvation to mankind through Jesus' death and resurrection. Jesus' second coming will mark the end of the Tribulation and the start of the 1000-year Millennium.

There is widespread belief among Orthodox Christians that the name Jesus is not merely a sequence of identifying symbols but includes intrinsic divine power.

"You will conceive and give birth to a son, and you are to call him Jesus. He will be great and will be called the Son of the Most High. The Lord God will give him the throne of his father David, and he will reign over Jacob's descendants forever; his kingdom will never end" (Luke 1:31–33).

"The angel answered, *"The Holy Spirit will come on you, and the power of the Most High will overshadow you. So the holy one to be born will be called the Son of God"* (Luke 1:35).

The Holy Spirit

Also known as the Third Person of the Trinity, the Holy Spirit works in the hearts of all people everywhere. Jesus told the disciples that He would send the Spirit into the world to *"convict the world of guilt in regard to sin and righteousness and judgment"* (John 16:7–11).

The Spirit applies the truths of God to the minds of men to convince them by fair and sufficient arguments that they are sinners. Responding to that conviction brings a person to salvation. The path to receiving the Holy Ghost is to exercise faith in Christ unto repentance. *"But the Helper, the Holy Spirit, whom the Father will send in My name, He will teach you all things, and bring to your remembrance all that I said to you"* (John 14:26).

"When the Helper comes, whom I will send to you from the Father, that is the Spirit of truth who proceeds from the Father, He will testify about Me" (John 15:26).

*Note: The Holy Spirit is equally God and possesses all the attributes of God. The Holy Spirit will be present and active during the Tribulation and will help bring those to faith in Christ. He will assist those Tribulation believers and seal and protect the 144,000 Jewish evangelists and the Two Witnesses. Regeneration is His work, and without Him, no one would be saved. Regeneration is rebirth or being born again.

The Holy Trinity

In biblical Orthodox Christian theology, this means the unity of the Father, the Son, and the Holy Spirit as three persons in one Godhead. The doctrine of the Trinity is one of the central biblical Christian affirmations about God. The Father, Son, and Holy Spirit were associated in New Testament passages such as the Great Commission: *"Go therefore and make disciples of all nations, baptizing them in the name of the Father and of the Son and of the Holy Spirit"* (Matthew 28:19).

In the apostolic benediction: *"The grace of the Lord Jesus Christ, the love of God, and the communion of the Holy Spirit be with you all"* (2 Corinthians 13:13).

The Bible

The Bible contains 66 books, written over 1500 years by over 40 authors from all walks of life. It is divided into two major sections: the Old and New Testaments.

The Bible is the holy scripture of the Christian religion. It tells the history of the Earth from its creation to the spread of Christianity in the first century A.D.

The Devil

Known as the Prince of evil spirits and adversary of God. The devil is also referred to as Satan, and is best known as the personification of evil and the destroyer of good people. He has been called many names in various cultures, such as Lucifer and Beelzebub.

Satan has been presented with various physical descriptions, including horns and hooved feet, and was given dominance over this earth. This is his kingdom. The Bible states that the Devil was once a most beautiful angel named Lucifer, but defied God and was cast out of heaven with other fallen angels. In Christian theology, the devil's main task is that of tempting humans to reject the way of life and redemption and to accept the way of an evil world, which leads to death and destruction.

The Antichrist (Beast)

Satan's Superman during the end times. He will be a charismatic and eloquent leader, speak blasphemies, and be strikingly attractive, cunning, and cruel. The Antichrist's first treacherous act will be to make peace with Israel that will last 3 1/2 years (the first half of the Tribulation period). He will be killed, and Satan will bring him back to life (counterfeit resurrection of Jesus). His False Prophet associate will initiate the Mark of the Beast. The Antichrist will desecrate the rebuilt temple in Jerusalem (abomination of desolation), and he will attempt to kill all Jews.

The False Prophet

He is referred to as the "Second Beast" (Revelation 13:11). The False Prophet comes up out of the earth, which could mean he is coming from the pit of hell, or it could mean that he is unknown until he bursts on the world stage at the right hand of the Antichrist. He will have persuasive words that elicit sympathy and goodwill from people and will deceive many. His mission is to force humanity to worship the Antichrist, and he is empowered by Satan.

Mark of the Beast

Initiated by the False Prophet, the mark is placed on the right hand or forehead. It represents the name of the Beast or the number of his name...666, the number of man. Those experiencing the terrors of the Tribulation will face two difficult choices. Those who refuse to accept the Mark of the Beast cannot buy or sell anything and will be subject to death (Revelation 13:15). Conversely, those who worship him will incur the wrath of God and face eternal fire and damnation at judgment time.

The Unholy Trinity

Satan is the first person and <u>Father</u>, the Antichrist is the second person and <u>Son</u>, and the False Prophet is the third person and Holy Spirit of the Unholy Trinity.

Hell

This is the consequence of sin and not believing in Jesus. ***The Lake of Fire*** (Hell) will be a place of perpetual suffering and misery. Scripture indicates that every person whose name is not in the *Book of Life* will be cast into the Lake of Fire (Revelation 20:15).

Some people think that Satan is the ruler of Hell. Not even close. God is in control of everything. For every word Jesus spoke about heaven, He said three about hell. The Bible references that it is "down"—but no specific location. It is a place of torment and flames, wailing and gnashing of teeth, where the worm does not die, and the fire is not quenched. It is a molten lake of fire and brimstone, and the destination of all who have rebelled against God for all time.

Only a few verses near the end of the book of Revelation use the term "Lake of Fire" (Revelation 19:20; 20:10; 14; 15; 21:8). Jesus also refers to Gehenna several times (Matthew 10:28; Mark 9:43; Luke 12:5) and an "outer darkness" (Matthew 8:12; 22:13). These all seem to be different references to the same thing—**Hell**. The Bible emphasizes not any degree of punishment in Hell but the importance of avoiding it altogether.

The Rapture

"For the Lord himself will descend from heaven with a cry of command, with the archangel's call, and with the sound of the trumpet of God. And the dead in Christ will rise first; then we who are alive, who are left, shall be caught up together with them in the clouds to meet the Lord in the air; and so we shall always be with the Lord" (1 Thessalonians 4:16–17).

Some wonder where the idea of the Rapture comes from, considering that the word "Rapture" does not appear in English translations. Our English word Rapture derives from the Latin word "rapio", which translates to the Greek **"harpazo"** (to catch up or carry away (1 Thessalonians 4:17).

God's redemptive plan is to restore what was lost in the Garden of Eden with Adam and Eve and to restore a proper relationship with him. However, before the establishment of the Messianic kingdom at Christ's return, God will pour his wrath out upon the world opposed to his rule. Many think the Church will be protected from this wrath by being raptured to heaven.

During the rapture of the Church, we will receive a body like unto His body that can never die, grow old or fail: *"Flesh and blood cannot inherit the kingdom of God, and the perishable cannot inherit the imperishable. Believers will be changed, in the twinkling of an eye at the last trumpet"* (1 Cor. 15:49–55).

*Note: The Bible speaks of three classes of people—Jews, Gentiles, and the church of God (1 Corinthians 10:32). Until Abraham's time, all people were Gentiles. When God called Abraham to begin a new nation, Abraham became the first Hebrew, Jew, or Israelite. The church is the body of Christ, which started on the Day of Pentecost and will go to heaven in the Rapture. It is only composed of saved Jews and Gentiles.

What Will the Rapture Be Like? If we use Jesus' resurrection as an example, our physical body will be transformed from temporal to eternal:

> "I will greatly rejoice in the Lord; my soul shall exult in my God, for he has clothed me with the garments of salvation; he has covered me with the robe of righteousness, as a bridegroom decks himself like a priest with a beautiful headdress, and as a bride adorns herself with her jewels" (Isaiah 61:10).

I can't see much of our jewelry, watches, etc. following us to Heaven, but who knows? Since our bodies will be like Jesus's, perhaps we can even pass from one dimension to another. After we are raptured, the earth will begin to experience a series of catastrophic events.

Imagine if you will, the destruction and chaos that will occur when this event happens. Pilots flying commercial and private aircraft will suddenly disappear from the cockpit. Surgeons performing operations will be whisked away, freeways will be blocked with horrible accidents, and many people will suddenly be gone. Unborn babies will disappear from their mothers' womb, children at the school playground will disappear, and no one will be left on this planet but unbelievers and Satan's followers. People will be desperately looking for a leader during this time, but unfortunately, the only one who will promise peace and support will be the Antichrist.

Those asking why a loving God would do all this need to remember that God sent His only Son to die on a cross so that we could have eternal life with Him in a New Heaven and a New Earth. All we must do is put our faith in Jesus Christ and obey His commands.

Marriage Supper of the Lamb

This symbolizes the union between Christ and the Church: *"Let us be glad and rejoice, and give honour to him: for the marriage of the Lamb is come, and his wife hath made herself ready. And to her was granted that she should be arrayed in fine linen, clean and white: for the fine linen is the righteousness of saints. And he saith unto me, Write, Blessed are they which are called unto the marriage supper of the Lamb. And he saith unto me, These are the true sayings of God"* (Revelation 19:7–9).

Judgment Seat of Christ (The Bema)

This will occur in heaven for believers to give an account of their works and hopefully receive rewards. The rewards (***crowns***) are based on our faithfulness in serving Him. These rewards will glorify Jesus, and we will lay them down before His feet as a tribute to the One who created and saved us. Everything good and right comes to us through the Lord, so surely, He deserves our crowns (Revelation 4:10).

The crowns we are hoping to receive are:

Crown of Incorruption: The Incorruptible Crown is also known as the Imperishable Crown (1 Corinthians 9:25). This crown is given to those individuals who demonstrate self-denial and perseverance, and have lived a disciplined life.

Crown of Life: This is also called the Martyr's Crown (James 1:12 and Revelation 2:10) and is bestowed upon "those who persevere under trials." It will be given to people who have stayed true to Christ's course while dealing with adversity.

Crown of Rejoicing: This is also known as the Crown of Exultation, or Crown of Auxiliary (1 Thess. 2:19 and Phil. 4:1), and is given to people who engage in evangelism of those outside the Christian Church.

Crown of Glory: Given to those faithful ministering the Word. Those who "shepherd the flock in unselfish love, being a good example to others" (1 Peter 5:24).

Crown of Righteousness: is a reward waiting for those who lived righteously while facing temptation and hardships on earth (2 Timothy 1:12). This crown is also promised to "those who love and anticipate" the Second Coming of Christ (2 Timothy 4:8).

Crowns symbolize authority, so they denote the authority given to Christians during the Millennial period when they will reign with Christ for 1000 years. Regardless of what crowns we may receive here on this earth, nothing will compare to the crowns awaiting us in Heaven, which can then be cast before our Lord's feet (Revelation 4:1).

The Tribulation

The Bible refers to a seven-year period as the Tribulation. The second 3 ½ year period is called the Great Tribulation because the Antichrist will be revealed, and the wrath of God will intensify.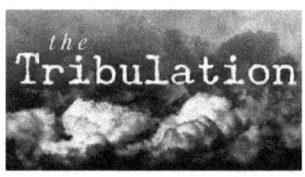

> "*I have said these things to you, that in me you may have peace. In the world you will have tribulation. But take heart; I have overcome the world*" (John 16:33).

> **"For then there will be great tribulation, such as has not been from the beginning of the world until now, no, and never will be"** (Matthew 24:21).

> "Jesus said, '*Immediately after the tribulation of those days shall the sun be darkened, and the moon shall not give her light, and the stars shall fall from heaven, and the powers of the heavens shall be shaken. And then shall appear the sign of the Son of man in heaven: and then shall all the tribes of the earth mourn, and they shall see the Son of man coming in the clouds of heaven with power and great glory*" (Matthew 24:29-30).

After the Rapture, all believers of Christ will have left the planet, and untold evil will be released. Can you imagine the terror and chaos on Earth? People will cry out looking for someone who can help, and the Antichrist and the False Prophet will offer false help. The Tribulation will be one of the most horrible times.

The purpose of the Tribulation is to call Israel back into her covenant relationship with her King and cause her to cry out in desperation (2 Chronicles 7:14). The Tribulation will force mankind to receive or reject Christ.

There will be a great harvest of souls during the Tribulation, and the gospel will be preached worldwide. The Two Witnesses will accomplish this along with the 144,000

Israelis and the Silent Witness—the Bible. In the Tribulation period, thousands of Jews on earth will be slaughtered, all killed for the word of God and the testimony of Jesus Christ.

A Prayer for Times of Tribulation: "Lord, we're living in perilous times. The kingdoms are in an uproar. The nation of Israel sits at the hub of history, and the predictions of Your Word are unfolding like a scroll. Evil has never been stronger, and the end has never been closer. Our world is in the grip of the birth pangs of tribulation, the likes of which have never been seen before and will never be seen again. Lord, rejecting the spirit of fear, we claim the Spirit of power, love, and a sound mind. Help us preach the gospel in these last days. Give us a sense of urgency, anticipation, and evangelism as we await the upward call. May we persevere as we listen for the shout, for the voice of the archangel, and for the trumpet call of God. Dear Lord, give us patience and give us power. Give us strength and sound minds, as we pray: 'Even so, come, Lord Jesus!" —*Dr. David Jeremiah*

Two Witnesses

Two Witnesses (possibly Moses and Elijah) will emerge at the start of the Tribulation. They will have power and prophesy for 1260 days (42 months) and be dressed in sackcloth. There will be two because this complies with Jewish law's legal standards.

They will be greatly hated because they tell people the disasters are judgments for rejecting Jesus as Lord. They can produce fire from their mouth to those wanting to harm them. They can cause drought, death, and every kind of plague. After 42 months, when their ministry is completed, God will allow the Antichrist to kill them. Their bodies will lie in the street with people rejoicing for 3 1/2 days, and then the breath of life from God will enter them, and they will suddenly stand for all to see. A cloud will envelop them, and they will rise to heaven. A large earthquake will then strike Jerusalem.

The 144,000
These are specially chosen pure Jewish evangelists—12,000 witnesses from each of the 12 tribes of Israel (12000 x 12000 = 144,000). The living God seals them on their foreheads, and as servants of God, they will be protected as they evangelize throughout the Tribulation. They will be with Jesus at the end of the Tribulation on Mount Zion. A great multitude of people will be saved and washed in Jesus's blood.

The "Silent Witness"
Millions of copies of the Bible will remain available on Earth.

An Angel Sent By God
God will send a specific angel during the Tribulation:

> "And I saw another angel fly in the midst of heaven, having the everlasting gospel to preach unto them that dwell on the earth, and to every nation, and kindred, and tongue, and people, Saying with a loud voice, Fear God, and give glory to him; for the hour of his judgment is come: and worship him that made heaven, and earth, and the sea, and the fountains of waters" (Revelation 14:6).

The Tribulation Saints
These are the significant number of people who will place their faith in Jesus Christ during the Tribulation. However, there are probably few that will survive until the Millennium. In his vision of heaven, John sees a vast number of these saints whom the Antichrist has martyred:

> "There before me was a great multitude that no one could count, from every nation, tribe, people and language, standing before the throne and in front of the Lamb. They were wearing white robes and were holding palm branches in their hands" (Revelation 7:9).

When John asks who they are, he is told, *"These are they who have come out of the great tribulation; they have washed their robes and made them white in the blood of the Lamb"* (verse 14).

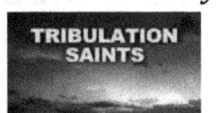

Battle of Armageddon

Armageddon is the Mount of Slaughter (*Hebrew – Mount Megiddo*). This battle will make all wars to date look like minor skirmishes, and ALL nations will be involved. The **Antichrist** will be the leader, and his purpose is to annihilate the Jews and to fight Christ and his army. The battle will take place on an extended plain from the Mediterranean Sea to the northern part of Israel at the foot of Mount Megiddo. This is about 55 miles north of Jerusalem and 10 miles from Nazareth. In 1799, Napoleon stood here and said there was no place in the world more suited for war.

The book of Revelation states that in this battle, *"blood came up to the horse's bridles for 1600 furlongs"* (200 miles—about the distance from the northern to southern tip of the land of Israel). Those nations that have persecuted the Jewish people so much will be finally gathered in the Valley of Jehoshaphat.

Step by step, the Antichrist will promote himself from a European leader to a world leader, to a tyrannical global dictator, and finally to a god. The world will become discontented, and major forces will assemble and rebel against him. The King of the South will come first, followed by the armies of the North to challenge this world dictator. The Antichrist will fight this rebellion, but bad news from the East and North will trouble him. The 6th angel pours out his bowl of wrath on the Euphrates River, and its water dries up. Massive armies now start coming over the dried river against him. The number of horsemen in the army was 200 million. The Antichrist must now divert much of his attention to this army instead of the South and North armies. It's hard to imagine the scene, but now there will be human armies and an innumerable host of supernatural beings. All the world's armies will descend on this plain for the epic battle. About the time that the Antichrist is going to attack and destroy Israel and Jerusalem, the Lord will appear with all His saints and angels to reclaim the world:

> *"The heaven will open and behold a white horse; and he that sat upon him was called* **Faithful and True**, *and in righteousness he doth judge and make war. His eyes were as a flame of fire, and on his head were many crowns; and he had a name written, that no man knew, but he himself. And he was clothed with a vesture dipped in blood: and his name is called The Word of God. And the armies which were in heaven followed him upon white horses, clothed in fine linen, white and clean. And out of his mouth goeth a sharp sword, that with it he should smite the nations: and he shall rule them with a rod of iron: and he treadeth the winepress of the fierceness and wrath of Almighty God. And he hath on his vesture and on his thigh a name written* **'King of Kings and Lord Of Lords**.*"*

In his arrogance and hatred for the Son of God, the Antichrist will turn his armies to engage Jesus (Revelation 19:19). The Antichrist and the kings of the earth will make war with Jesus. The Antichrist's armies will be slain by the sword of Him that sat upon the horse. Jesus will then snatch up the Antichrist and the False Prophet and fling them into the Lake of Fire. The Antichrist and False Prophet will get to Hell before Satan, who joins them at the end of the Millennium.

The Tribulation Ends

> *"And I saw an angel come down from heaven, having the key of the bottomless pit and a great chain in his hand. And he laid hold on the dragon, that old serpent, which is the Devil, and Satan, and bound him a thousand years, and cast him*

into the bottomless abyss. He should deceive the nations no more, till the thousand years should be fulfilled: and after that he must be loosed a little season" (Revelation 20:1-3).

The Millennium Begins

The Millennium Kingdom is the future 1000-year reign of Jesus Christ on earth as He sits on David's throne in Jerusalem. God will redeem everyone who enters that kingdom and is righteous (Isaiah 35:8-10). Two distinct groups of people will be among the redeemed: those with glorified physical bodies and those with natural, earthly bodies.

Those with glorified bodies will be the Church, whose bodies were either resurrected or changed at the Rapture. Tribulation Martyrs are resurrected after Christ returns to earth (Revelation 20:4-6), and the Old Testament Saints may also be resurrected at this time (Daniel 12:2).

Those who occupy the kingdom with earthly bodies are the surviving and believing Gentiles and Jews. Many of them will have children during this kingdom's reign, but unfortunately, many of the children will choose not to believe in Jesus. Remember that those born in the kingdom will be sinners at birth since they are still descendants of Adam (Romans 5:12-14, 16-19).

The primary purpose of the Millennium is the restoration of Israel and Christ's rule over it, but it is also designed to:

1. Reward the people of God,

2. Respond to the Prophet's Predictions,

3. For Jesus to reign as the acknowledged King over the House of Jacob and,

4. To fulfill The Lord's Prayer (or Disciples' Prayer): *Thy kingdom come, thy will be done on earth as it is in heaven* (Luke 11:2-4).

Millennium Ends

At the end of Christ's thousand-year reign on earth, Satan is released from the abyss. The seemingly perfect environment of the Millennium does not guarantee an ideal relationship with God. No matter how much proof, evidence, or experience people are given, some will never submit to God.

As soon as Satan is released, he resumes his intense opposition to God and God's people. Many unbelievers will be living at the end of the 1000 years since Revelation 20:7-10 prophesies that people from the nations of the world will join Satan in a final war against God.

Satan's massive assault on Jerusalem fails because fire comes down from heaven and consumes the armies. Satan is then cast into the Lake of Fire with the Antichrist and the False Prophet, and they will suffer torment forever (Revelation 19:20).

The Great White Throne Judgment

Unbelievers of all ages will be resurrected and stand before Jesus at the Great White Throne Judgment. Each will be judged, and those whose names are not written in Lamb's *Book of Life* will be thrown into the **Lake of Fire**, a place of everlasting punishment (Revelation 20:15).

The Bible states that unbelievers are storing up wrath against themselves and that God will "*give to each person according to what he has done*" (Romans 2:5-6). In their resurrected bodies, unbelievers will live forever in this burning lake, which is "*the second death*" (Rev 20:14). The Lake of Fire's specific location is never given in scripture, but we may be given a clue:

> "Then another angel, a third one, followed them, saying with a loud voice: "*If anyone worships the beast and his image, and receives a mark on his forehead or on his hand, he also will drink of the wine of the wrath of God, which is*

mixed in full strength in the cup of His anger; and he will be tormented with fire and brimstone in the presence of the holy angels and in the presence of the Lamb" (Revelation 14:9).

Notice that the place of eternal torment is "in the presence of the holy angels and in the presence of the Lamb." Could this imply that the Lake of Fire will be located in a heavenly place, rather than in the physical realm? Could this be a burning sun?

The Kingdom

Jesus will hand over the kingdom to God the Father after he has abolished all rule, authority, and power (1 Corinthians 15:23-24). Jesus has always been submissive to the Father and was sent to earth to provide atonement for sin, fulfill prophecy, teach the way of righteousness, and defeat Satan and his work.

We are reminded of God's curse on the serpent and his promise of a future conflict and victory between the woman's offspring and the serpent (Genesis 3:15). Jesus is the Father's instrument of action, to save sinners caught in the serpent's snares and to establish the perfect Kingdom throughout all creation.

"The kingdom of the world has become the kingdom of our Lord and of his Messiah, and He will reign for ever and ever" (Revelation 11:15).

"And I heard a loud voice from the throne saying, Now the dwelling of God is with men, and he will live with them. They will be his people, and God himself will be with them and be their God. He will wipe every

tear from their eyes. There will be no more death or mourning or crying or pain, for the old order of things has passed away" (Revelation 21).

The new earth and the new heavens are sometimes called the *"eternal state."*

> *"The day of the Lord will come like a thief, and then the heavens will pass away with a roar, and the heavenly bodies will be burned up and dissolved, and the earth and the works that are done on it will be exposed"* (2 Peter 3:10).

There are several different opinions about the Earth being destroyed. Could it be that God uses fire to destroy all on Earth, or just all the Earth that displeases Him? And that which pleases Him would endure the fire and be reconstructed? Scripture states that the present earth will *"pass away"* or be *"laid bare."* Could this also be interpreted as *"changed"* or *"renewed?"*

Some think the Lord will not destroy the earth but reconstruct the old heaven and earth. This might be compared to the Flood of Noah's time, when the world was not destroyed but cleansed and purified by the flood.

In the new world, sin will be eradicated, and "there shall be no more curse" (Revelation 22:3). This refers to the words God spoke to Adam and Eve in the Garden of Eden.

The scripture states that there will be no more sea: "And I saw a new heaven and a new earth: for the first heaven and the first earth were passed away; and there was no more sea" (Revelation 21:1).

About 71 percent of the Earth's surface is covered with water, and the oceans hold about 96.5 percent of all water. The Bible says there will be no more seas; however, that doesn't necessarily mean we won't have beautiful bodies of water. Perhaps we won't have large wastelands of salty seas.

However, another interpretation of this statement is "no more seas." Throughout the Bible, there are references to the sea representing the potential for evil. The sea is a picture of dangerous instability because it is shapeless and formless. No longer having a sea may mean there will no longer be any potential for evil or for anyone to fall anew into sin because it has been removed.

A significant feature of the new earth will be the **Holy City, "New Jerusalem."** It will come down from heaven and be God's dwelling place among the people. Heaven is God's home. Earth is our home. Jesus Christ as God/man forever links God and mankind and, therefore, links Heaven and Earth. There will be one universe, with all things in Heaven and on Earth together under one head, Jesus Christ.

Holy City: New Jerusalem

This is called the Celestial City—*Mount Zion* (the place where **Yahweh**, the God of Israel, dwells (Isaiah 8:18; Gal. 4; Revelation 21). The great city of New Jerusalem will come down out of heaven and become the capital city of God's eternal kingdom. Upon resurrection, individuals will inhabit the Earth in their renewed bodies with an eternal existence with Christ.

There will be no Temple in the New Jerusalem because the Lord God and the Lamb are its temple. In Moses' day, God established the Tabernacle, and He dwelt with the people in what was known as the Holy of Holies. While Solomon reigned, this was transferred to the Temple, but then God departed the Temple because of Israel's apostasy. Then Jesus Christ came to become the complete and final sacrifice.

A Temple will be provided during the Millennial kingdom to memorialize Jesus' redemptive work in the prior age. In the eternal order, a Temple will be unnecessary, as God, Jesus Christ, and the Holy Spirit will be present.

Description: The city is holy and has a great wall that measures one hundred and forty-four cubits and is made of jasper. The twelve foundations of the wall are adorned with precious stones, and in them were found the names of the twelve apostles of Christ. There are twelve gates. Each is made of a single pearl—three on the north, south, east, and west. The city is like pure gold.

The surface area of our current Earth is about 197 million square miles. Around 57 million square miles (29%) is covered by land, while the remaining 140 million square miles (71%) are covered by water. Randy Alcorn has some fascinating statistics regarding New Jerusalem City.

An angel measured the city's size, which is reported to be the equivalent of 1,400 miles in length, width, and height, and these are given in man's measurements. If in the middle of the United States, this city would stretch from Canada to Mexico, and from the Appalachian Mountains to the California border. The ground level of the city would be nearly two million square feet. If this 1,400-mile cube consists of multiple stories, and if each story has a 12-foot ceiling, the city could have over 600,000 stories. There will be no need for the sun (or moon) to shine because the glory of God will illuminate everything. The Lamb will provide the light.

The *River of the Water of Life* represents the eternal life and abundant blessings that flow from God to His people. The *Tree of Life* stands in the middle of the street and by the River, and it bears 12 types of fruit monthly. Its leaves are for healing nations: *"And he that sat upon the throne said, Behold, I make all things new. And he said unto me, Write: for these words are true and faithful. And he said unto me, It is done. I am Alpha and Omega, the beginning and the end. I will give unto him that is athirst of the fountain of the water of life freely. He that overcometh shall inherit all things; and I will be his God, and he shall be my son."*

Eternity Begins

Eternity is defined as infinite, endless, forever, and timeless.

"For God so loved the world, that He gave His only begotten Son, that whoever believes in Him shall not perish, but have eternal life."

This old earth was never meant to be our final destination in God's plan. It is only a detour to allow His creation an opportunity to choose eternity with Him in the new world.

As I look back at scripture, it is apparent that God created us for companionship. God wanted us to be His companions willingly and to choose Him. We have two options with our free will. The first is to believe in God's plan and Jesus Christ as our savior. The second option is to deny Jesus and follow Satan's worldly ways in a life of sin and an eternal death in the Lake of Fire.

Part II: Those Fascinating Things in the Bible

Unicorns

The unicorn (u-na-corn) is a legendary creature described since antiquity as a beast (horse or goat) with a single large, pointed, spiraling horn projecting from its forehead. In the Middle Ages and Renaissance, its horn was described as having the power to render poisoned water potable and to heal sickness. So, what does that have to do with the Bible?

Well, the King James version, first printed in the early 17th century, mentions the word unicorn in several passages, (Numbers 23:22; 24:8; Deuteronomy 33:17; Job 39:9–10; Psalms 22:21; 29:6; and Isaiah 34:7). In these passages, it is believed that "unicorn" does not mean the supernatural animals we know today, but refers to a horned animal, symbolizing power and strength. When scholars translated the Bible's Old Testament from Hebrew to Greek, they encountered a large and powerful animal called the "re'em," translated as *monokeros* in the Septuagint and *unicornis* in the Latin Vulgate. Later versions use the phrase "wild ox."

The original Hebrew word basically means "beast with a horn." Over time this word was translated as "*unicorn*" in the King James Version. Some scholars believe the creature being talked about is either the "*oryx*," a large African and Arabian antelope, the "*aurochs*," an extinct cattle species, or perhaps even better, the "*monokeros*," meaning rhinoceros. The KJV scriptures chose to substitute "unicorn" for the name of this horned animal each time it occurred.

It is much disputed among the learned whether this "reem" could be the rhinoceros, Arabian buffalo, wild bull, or wild goat. However, keep in mind that its characteristics are:

(1) Great Strength, (2) It cannot be Tamed or Trained, (3) Its strength was in its Horn or Horns, and (4) The special majesty or dignity in the horns of this animal attracted attention and made it the Symbol of Dominion.

However, early colonists in South Africa discovered ancient rock art in the area that featured unicorn-like animals. Could these be the legendary creature called the unicorn? The following are some of the Bible scriptures that mention the unicorn:

- God's might that took His people out of Egypt is likened to a unicorn's (Numbers 23:22).

- The Lord's power is again related to that of a unicorn and is described as being strong enough to eat up the adversaries of His people and break their bones (Numbers 24:8).

- The slaughter of the wicked nations as a sacrifice of wild animals (Isaiah 34:7). The verse mentions wild oxen, young bulls, and <u>unicorns</u> as the animals that will be killed.

- *"Save me from the lion's mouth: for thou hast heard me from the <u>horns of the unicorns</u>"* (Psalms 22:21). This verse explains David's lamentations as he cries for help and deliverance from his overpowering enemies, whom he calls "the horn of a unicorn."

- *"He maketh them also to skip like a calf; Lebanon and Sirion <u>like a young unicorn</u>"* (Psalms 29:6).

- The power of Joseph is like a <u>bullock with the horns of a unicorn</u> to denote great strength and power (Deuteronomy 33:17).

- *"Will the <u>unicorn</u> be willing to serve thee, or abide by thy crib? Can you bring it into subjection to your command?"* (Job 39:9).

Leviathan, the Sea Monster

(le-vi-a-than) Leviathan is a sea creature that appears in the Old Testament to symbolize God's power over creation and Israel's enemies. Leviathan is sometimes described as a multiheaded serpent, a whale-like creature, or a fire-breathing crocodile that lives in the depths of the ocean —the watery abyss.

So, is this Old Testament sea monster a creature that lived or a fictional animal used for symbolism? The Bible states that it's real and is a strong, armor-plated creature with many teeth and the ability to breathe fire from its mouth.

"Out of his mouth go burning lamps, and sparks of fire leap out. Out of his nostrils goeth smoke, as out of a seething pot or caldron" (Job 41:1-34). God's authority over creation is emphasized in these scriptures.

"There go the ships: there is that leviathan, whom thou hast made to play therein" (Psalms 104:26). The sight of it will terrify anyone, and it is powerful enough to churn up the sea. It is far too strong for people to capture, and God formed Leviathan to "frolic" in the deep sea.

Some think the ships symbolize the church and God's people navigating the world, facing trials and tribulations. Then, perhaps symbolically, the Leviathan represents Satan and reminds us of spiritual battles and the need for vigilance.

"Thou brakest the heads of leviathan in pieces, and gavest him to be meat to the people inhabiting the wilderness" (Psalms 74:14).

This verse highlights God's power and sovereignty. Some say this leviathan metaphor refers to the Egyptian government, whose heads represent Pharaoh and his chief captains. The second part may refer to the defeated leviathan (Egypt) becoming sustenance for the creatures in the wilderness, possibly referring to birds and beasts of prey.

"In that day the Lord with his sore and great and strong sword shall punish leviathan the piercing serpent, even leviathan that crooked serpent; and he shall slay the dragon that is in the sea" (Isaiah 27:1). This verse may symbolize Israel's enemies and their eventual defeat. Some say that the Lord's Sword is the Word of God, while others see it as divine judgment. Perhaps the leviathan symbolizes earthly rulers or oppressive powers such as Egypt, Babylon, or Rome. The dragon in the sea could likely refer to Satan, the ultimate enemy.

Many cultures have legends of sea monsters, including the civilizations of Egypt and Mesopotamia near Israel. Ancient people believed the leviathan to be the cause of solar eclipses. They thought that the sun was covered because the leviathan used to eat it for that period. Leviathan, the serpent, is the most common symbol of Satanism. The ritual *"raising the serpent"* brings awareness, enlightenment, and psychic abilities. Leviathan represents various themes in the Bible, including God's power, authority, and victory over adversaries. So, what do you think, is the leviathan a real fire-breathing sea creature?

The Nephilim

Nephilim (neph-a-lim) appears in the Bible twice: once in Genesis 6:16 and again in Numbers 13:33.

In the Old Testament, Nephilim were mysterious beings or people of considerable size and strength who lived before and after the Flood. They are said to be the children of the *"sons of God"* and the *"daughters of man."*

Their origins are disputed, but some view them as the offspring of fallen angels and humans.

"When human beings began to increase in number on the earth and daughters were born to them, the sons of God saw that the daughters of humans were beautiful, and they

married any of them they chose. Then the LORD *said, "My Spirit will not contend with humans forever, for they are mortal; their days will be a hundred and twenty years." The Nephilim were on the earth in those days—and also afterward—when the sons of God went to the daughters of humans and had children by them. They were the heroes of old, men of renown"* (Genesis 6:1-6).

So, who are the sons of God? One theory is that they were fallen angels (demons) who took on physical form and mated with human females (or demons who possessed human males who then mated with human females), resulting in extraordinary offspring. If demons were involved in producing the Nephilim, God likely judged those demons, and they are now kept in darkness, bound with everlasting chains for judgment on the great day.

"And the angels who did not keep their positions of authority but abandoned their proper dwelling—these he has kept in darkness, bound with everlasting chains for judgment on the great Day" (Jude 6).

Perhaps the most information about the angels who sinned is found in 2 Peter 2:4. While the sin they committed is not described, their punishment is explained:

"For if God did not spare angels when they sinned, but sent them to hell, putting them in chains of darkness to be held for judgment."

So why would demons want to cohabit with human women and produce offspring? Perhaps it was an attempt to pollute the human bloodline to prevent the coming of the Messiah. God had promised that the Messiah would one day crush the head of the serpent, Satan. The demons were possibly attempting to prevent the crushing of the serpent and make it impossible for a sinless "seed of the woman" to be born.

The Bible doesn't explicitly say how these giants came to be. It's probably not that important in the grand scheme of things, but I assure you that they existed. Just ask David ... he met one named Goliath.

Behemoth

(be-he-moth) As God speaks to Job, this creature is described as a very large animal:

"It eats grass as an ox and his strength is in his loins, and his force is in the navel of his belly. He moveth his tail like a cedar: the sinews of his stones are wrapped together. His bones are as strong pieces of brass; his bones are like bars of iron. He is the chief of the ways of God: he that made him can make his sword to approach unto him. Surely the mountains bring him forth food, where all the beasts of the field play. He lieth under the shady trees, in the covert of the reed, and fens. The shady trees cover him with their shadow; the willows of the brook compass him about. Behold, he drinketh up a river, and hasteth not: he trusteth that he can draw up Jordan into his mouth. He taketh it with his eyes: his nose pierceth through snares" (Job 40:15–24).

God's description of this animal focuses on its great size and strength compared to Job's smallness and human frailty. Modern language has picked up on the biblical description and uses the word behemoth to mean *"anything of monstrous size or power."* The behemoth is described as unstoppable and fearless. It is a plant-eating animal that lives near water and is at home even in a flooded, raging river. It is powerful and muscular. Only its Creator can master it. It has a massive tail that *"sways like a cedar,"* and hunting the behemoth is futile because it cannot be captured.

The Hebrew word for behemoth is *"bəhēmōth,"* meaning "beast." Some scholars believe it refers to the elephant, hippopotamus, or water-ox. We do not know what unstoppable and fearless creature was being described to Job, but the cedar-like tail hardly fits the stubby or rope-like tails of the elephant, hippopotamus, or water-ox. However, the crocodile seems to have many of these characteristics, especially a cedar-like tail.

Or perhaps it was a type of *dinosaur* such as the *diplodocus or apatosaurus*. Some of these were the largest of all land animals, were marsh-loving plant-eaters, had tails like trees, and could be called *"kings" of the animals."* Would the dinosaur still be around in Job's day? The behemoth was certainly no one's pet—except God's.

Cockatrice

The *cockatrice* is *a legendary monster myth (basilisk heraldry)*. A mythical animal with a cock's head (half-rooster and half-snake), with the ability to kill at a glance. In 1611, when the KJV was produced, the translators used the word "*cockatrice*" to translate the Hebrew word "*tsepha*," which means "poisonous serpent or viper." Cockatrices are mentioned by name four times in the King James Bible translation of the Old Testament, and once as an adder in Proverbs 23:32.

"*And the sucking child shall play on the hole of the asp, and the weaned child shall put his hand on the cockatrice den*" (Isaiah 11:8).

"*Rejoice not thou, whole Palestina, because the rod of him that smote thee is broken: for out of the serpent's root shall come forth a cockatrice, and his fruit shall be a fiery flying serpent*" (14:29).

"*They hatch cockatrice' eggs, and weave the spider's web: he that eateth of their eggs dieth, and that which is crushed breaketh out into a viper*" (59:5).

"For, behold, I will send serpents, cockatrices, among you, which will not be charmed, and they shall bite you, saith the LORD" (Jeremiah 8:17).

Today, we have a much better understanding of Hebrew and biology. This is why modern translations use the words "viper," "adder," and "poisonous snake" to translate the original Hebrew word, *"tsepha."*

Dragons

I am reminded not to end this study without mentioning this legendary beast. Most of us associate dragons with storybooks and medieval folklore, but "dragons" are mentioned at least thirty times in the King James Bible translation. Twenty-two of these matches are in the Old Testament, of which seventeen are derived from the Hebrew word *"tanniyn,"* meaning a huge creature, dragon, dinosaur, serpent, or sea monster. The remaining thirteen mentions of dragons in the Bible are found in the book of Revelation.

"Praise *the Lord from the earth, ye dragons, and all deeps*" (Psalms 148:7).

"*The beast of the field shall honour me, the dragons and the owls: because I give waters in the wilderness, and rivers in the desert, to give drink to my people, my chosen*" (Isaiah 43:20). "*Therefore I will wail and howl, I will go stripped and naked: I will make a wailing like the dragons, and mourning as the owls*" (Micah 1:8).

The dragons are often described as sea monsters, serpents, and sinister cosmic forces. In the Bible, the dragon (Satan) appears as the primal enemy of God and is used to display God's supremacy over all creatures and creation.

Some scholars suggest that there are two different dragons in the Bible—**Leviathan** in the Old Testament and **Satan** in the New Testament. **"He seized the dragon, that ancient serpent, who is the devil, or Satan, and bound him for a thousand years"** (Revelation 20:2).

Interestingly, nearly every major ancient culture has myths and legends about giant reptiles or dragons. Some of these legends suggest that humans and dragons or dinosaurs might have coexisted.

Many evolutionary experts theorize that dinosaurs existed millions of years before human beings. However, some young-earth creationists believe the "dragon" myths came from real contact between human beings and dinosaurs.

This view holds that all animals were created around 6,000 years ago and coexisted with human beings. That could explain why all human cultures have stories about giant reptiles—they may have actually seen them!

As mentioned previously, there is probably no other book published that is more amazing than the Bible. The people, the stories, the animals, and the symbolic interpretations are fascinating. The Bible is comprised of sixty-six different books, to which about 40 different human authors contributed, and it was written over a period of about 1500 years. Ultimately, it has one author—God Himself.

Part III: Miscellaneous Topics

Body, Spirit, Soul & Holy Spirit Revisited

A few years ago, I started my "white paper" studies, and the first one I did was a look at the Body, Spirit, and the Soul. I finished this study but was not 100% sure that I reached my goal of thoroughly understanding the biblical relationship of these three terms. To that end, I am refocusing on making it easier to understand. I will add to what I have done and other new thoughts and information regarding the Holy Spirit.

We learn that God formed man from the dust of the ground (formed the "<u>body</u>"), breathed into him the breath of life (the Hebrew word is "ruach," which literally means "<u>spirit</u>," and man became a living being (a <u>soul</u>) (Genesis 2:7).

 A good example is to picture three circles. The outer circle is the body, the next circle is the soul, and the inner circle is the spirit. The soul is the result of the body and spirit coming together.

The Body: This is your physical part that interacts with the world. Your body can be used for either sin or holiness. An important thing to remember is that a believer's body holds the Holy Spirit's presence.

> *"Don't you realize that your body is the temple of the Holy Spirit, who lives in you and was given to you by God? You do not belong to yourself"* (1 Corinthians 6:19).

Scripture states that your body belongs to God.

The Soul: George MacDonald, a Scottish author, poet, and Christian minister, stated, *"You don't have a soul; you are a soul and have a body."*

In the Old Testament, the Hebrew word *"nephesh"* is often translated as *"soul."* In the New Testament, the Greek word *"psyche"* denotes the soul. When God breathed the breath of life into Adam, the man became a *"living soul."*

Although the nature of the human soul is not perfectly clear, in Christian theology, the soul is the part of a person that is not physical and will last eternally after the body experiences death. It's been said that there are only two things that last forever: the Word of God and the souls of men (Mark 13:31). Both are imperishable. The soul is the center of our thoughts, representing our personality and identity.

The Bible repeatedly refers to people as souls. In the days of Noah, eight "souls" were saved from the flood water (1 Peter 3:20).

"Then they that gladly received his word were baptized: and the same day there were added unto them about three thousand souls" (Acts 2:41).

The word "soul" is mentioned over 700 times in the Bible. However, this number varies depending on the Bible version used.

The Human Spirit: The spirit is considered the part of us that can directly experience God's presence, receive revelation, and engage in true worship. It includes our faith, hope, love, character, and perseverance.

The spirit enables us to think, feel, create, and enjoy many things, such as music and art. And because of the human spirit, we have a "free will" that no other creature on earth has. **"The spirit returns back to God who gave it"** (Ecclesiastes 12:7).

The Bible describes the soul and spirit as closely related but separable parts of a person. Many scholars have the *"tripartite"* view of humans, meaning we are composed of body, soul, and spirit, with each element playing a vital role in our lives. The Hebrew word for "spirit" is *"ruah,"* and it appears 389 times in the Old Testament.

The Bible describes the Holy Spirit as fully God. Together with God the Father and the Son (Jesus Christ), the Holy Spirit is the third member of the Godhead or the Trinity. He has been present with the Father and the Son since before time began. The Holy Spirit is omniscient, eternal, and omnipresent. The terms "Holy Spirit" and "Holy Ghost" are often used interchangeably to refer to the third person of the Holy Trinity.

The Holy Spirit's role is to guide, teach, and sanctify believers. He helps them experience God's love and power and become "born again"—more like Jesus. He is the restrainer of man's sinfulness, and during the end times, he will restrain the power of the Antichrist and Satan. He also grants spiritual gifts to individuals for service. Jesus also referred to the Holy Spirit as the "Paraclete" (Greek), meaning *"comforter"* or *"advocate."*

The Holy Spirit works in the lives of unbelievers by convicting them of their sin and showing them their need for a Savior. Responding to that conviction brings them to Salvation. Upon accepting Jesus Christ as a believer, the Holy Spirit of God joins with your spirit in ways we cannot comprehend. When we allow the Spirit of God to lead our lives, the *"Spirit Himself testifies with our spirit that we are God's children"* (Romans 8:16). This permanent indwelling is referred to as the *"guarantee of our inheritance."*

The Holy Spirit gives believers wisdom so they can understand God's Word. From the outset, the Holy Spirit's arrival at **Pentecost** allowed the apostles to speak in various tongues and effectively communicate the gospel to a diverse audience. This event set the stage for the expansive reach of the Christian message.

When Jesus was baptized, the three members of the ***Trinity*** appeared, together yet distinct. As Jesus rose from the water, the Spirit fell upon Him like a dove, while the voice of the Father was heard from heaven, saying that He was pleased with His beloved Son (Mark 1:10-11).

Jesus stated that *blasphemy* against the Spirit will not be forgiven (Matthew 12:22-32). Blasphemy refers to a deliberate and unyielding rejection of the truth, as the Spirit represents truth itself. Grieving the Holy Spirit means you refuse to listen to the Holy Spirit's conviction in your life and choose to live a life of sin.

If we count both the Old and New Testaments, the term 'Holy Spirit' is used 94 times in the Bible.

So, what happens to you when you die?

Scripture states that when an **unbeliever** dies, the body goes into the grave, and the spirit and soul are sent to a holding area (some say Hades or Sheol) where they will remain until the final resurrection at the close of our Lord's Millennial Kingdom. All unbelievers will then be judged at the **Great White Throne Judgment** and join Satan and his demonic forces in the **Lake of Fire** (Hell) for an eternity of torment.

Scripture states that when a **believer** dies, his body goes into the grave, and his soul and spirit go immediately to be with the Lord. At the Resurrection, the body and soul/spirit will be joined, and the new and glorified body will be with the Lord forever. God has provided redemption through His only begotten Son— Jesus Christ.

"And there is salvation in no one else, for there is no other name under heaven given among men by which we must be saved."

"Jesus saith unto him, I am the way, the truth, and the life: no man cometh unto the Father, but by me."

Some think we might have an intermediate body before receiving our eternal, glorified body. A theological concept called the *"intermediate state"* speculates on what kind of body, if any, believers in heaven have while they wait for their physical bodies to be resurrected. There is no official answer to the intermediate body issue; however, they had bodies in the parable of Lazarus and the rich man. When Moses and Elijah met with Jesus on the Mount of Transfiguration, they were represented as having bodies. And the martyred dead in heaven are described as wearing robes and being before the throne of God (Revelation 6:9-11).

However, while we may not have a temporary body between our death and the Resurrection, we do know that eventually, all believers will receive glorified bodies. These bodies will be especially suited for an existence in the "eternal state"—the New Heavens and New Earth.

Scripture states that when believers die, their souls/spirits go immediately to be with the Lord. As Jesus was hanging on the cross, He told one of the criminals who was also crucified, "Truly, I say to you, today you will be with me in paradise" (Luke 23:39-43). He did not mention anything about purgatory or soul sleep. He said, "Today."

<u>Did Jesus have a soul</u>? Jesus was (and is) fully God and fully man. When the Son of God became incarnate, He took on a sinless human nature, including a truly human soul. Jesus shared many human experiences.

In his agony in the Garden of Gethsemane, Jesus said, "***My soul is overwhelmed with sorrow to the point of death***" (Matthew 26:38). And at one point Jesus spoke of his troubled soul and the sacrifice he is going to make, "***Now my soul is troubled, and what shall I say? 'Father, save me from this hour'? No, it was for this very reason I came to this hour***" (John 12:27). His crucifixion highlights the depth of his emotional and spiritual emotions that were endured.

In Matthew 10:28, Jesus warns his followers to <u>fear not those who can kill the body but cannot kill the soul</u>, suggesting a distinction between the physical and the spiritual aspects of human beings. You often see the soul mentioned when talking about salvation and eternal life.

Jesus possessed a soul (free from sin) that allowed him to experience human emotions and intellect while still being divine. Jesus' soul would bear the weight of human sin in the redemption of humankind.

Matthew 16:26 may tell it best: ***"For what will it profit a man if he gains the whole world and forfeits his soul? Or what shall a man give in return for his soul?"***

Final Thoughts:

Scriptures that mention the soul and spirit together include Hebrews 4:12; 1 Samuel 1:15; Job 7:11; and Isaiah 26:9. However, Thessalonians 5:23 seems to treat the body, soul, and spirit as distinct from each other:

"And the very God of peace sanctify you wholly; and I pray God your whole spirit and soul and body be preserved blameless unto the coming of our Lord Jesus Christ."

The bottom line, as mentioned above, is that the soul refers to the essence of a person and gives us our sense of identity as individuals. The spirit refers to a non-physical part of us that allows us to experience deep emotions, achieve goals, and connect with God. Even though I see the soul and spirit as different, in some cases, I see them as the same.

I started this study with a passage from Genesis, and I will end it in the same manner. We learn that God formed man from the dust of the ground (**body**), breathed into him the breath of life (**spirit**), and man became a living being (**soul**) (Genesis 2:7). The heavens declare the glory of God, and the skies proclaim the work of his hands. Through Him all things were made, without him nothing was made that has been made. So, as you enjoy this wonderful life, and your body, soul, and spirit that God has given you, do everything to glorify God.

The Gift of Growing Old

If you are a youngster, you always wish you were older. But as you grow older, you wish you were younger. The Bible presents growing old as a regular, natural part of life. There is honor in the aging process because growing old is typically accompanied by increased wisdom and experience.

In the book of Ecclesiastes, **Solomon** provides a look at aging and the issues related to it. People are born with a natural tendency to *"live for the moment,"* but as they get older, they realize the shortness of this life and try to do things that give them a legacy. This usually doesn't work. **Solomon hoped people would grow wiser in using their God-given time before they die.** People should take joyful advantage of all their gifts, talents, wisdom, and opportunities before all opportunity is gone. The true meaning of our life will only be realized at the final judgment when we receive our inheritance.

So, how old did people live in the early part of the bible? The 10 oldest people in the bible (Genesis 5:21-27) were:

1. Methuselah – 969 Years Old
2. Jared – 962 Years Old (18-21)
3. Noah – 950 Years Old (10)
4. Adam – 930 Years Old (4-5)
5. Seth – 912 Years Old (8)
6. Kenan (also spelled Cainan) – 910 Years Old (14)
7. Enos – 905 Years Old (11)
8. Mahalalel – 895 Years Old (17)
9. Lamech – 777 Years Old (31)
10. Enoch – 365 Years Old (23)

No one is sure why people in the early chapters of Genesis lived such long lives, but something happened after the global flood to shorten their lifespan. By the time of Moses, who lived 120 years, lifespans were much lower.

One theory for why the people in this time lived such long lives is based on the idea that a canopy of water *"above the firmament"* created a greenhouse effect and blocked much of the radiation that now hits the Earth, resulting in ideal living conditions. Many scholars do not accept this canopy theory. Others think that over time, because of sin, the human genetic code became increasingly corrupted, and human beings became more and more susceptible to death and disease. This would also have resulted in drastically reduced lifespans. After Moses, only Jehoiada grew old and full of days, and died when he was 130 years old (2 Chronicles 24:15).

"For all our days are passed away in thy wrath: we spend our years as a tale that is told. The days of our years are threescore years and ten; and if by reason of strength they be fourscore years, yet is their strength labour and sorrow; for it is soon cut off, and we fly away" (Psalms 90:9–10).

In the Bible, "**fourscore years**" means eighty years (four times twenty = eighty). The phrase above suggests that even if someone lives to be fourscore years old, their strength is still labor and sorrow, and life is short. However, in Exodus 7:7, we learn that *"Moses was eighty years old and Aaron eighty-three when they spoke to Pharaoh."* You might say that Moses was just starting one of the most exciting experiences of his life.

According to the Centers for Disease Control and Prevention (CDC), the average life expectancy for a man in the United States in 2024 was 74.8 years. The life expectancy for females in the United States was 80.2 years. The average global life expectancy was 73.3 years, which varies widely across world regions.

So why am I so interested in this aging process? Well, I recently reached the milestone in life of "fourscore," which means 80 years old. At 80, do I have to go on a "if it tastes horrible but is good for me" diet? I don't want to be one of those elderly people you hear about who were riding their exercise bikes and had a heart attack.

Regardless of what you read, there is nothing we can or cannot do that will guarantee us a long life. Only God knows the number of our days here on earth. You can do what the doctor says about eating right and exercising, and I am not against that. But then you always hear about the 100-year-old grandma that smokes four packs of cigarettes a day or the 97-year-old man that never exercises and drinks 10 soda pops or beers a day. Where is the justice?

What about my gray hair?

> "The glory of young men is their strength, but the splendor of old men is their gray hair" (Proverbs 20:29).

> "Gray hair is a crown of glory; it is gained in a righteous life" (Proverbs 16:31).

> "You shall stand up before the gray head and honor the face of an old man, and you shall fear your God: I am the Lord" (Leviticus 19:32).

(I never thought gray hair was a sign of glory).

So, what can an older person offer the world?

> "Is not wisdom found among the aged? Does not long-life bring understanding?" (Job 12:12).

An 80-year-old person has learned a great deal, and this wisdom is meant to be shared. Older generations are responsible for mentoring, encouraging, and guiding young people. Older men and women should teach and set an example for younger people. Their thoughts and experiences can be a source of strength for others.

So, is the best part of my life behind me, with nothing exciting to look forward to in the future? I think not.

<u>Remember that you are still alive today because of God's plan. He is not through with you yet.</u>

We are all challenged as we age, and health issues may arise. However, Isaiah reminds us that God's strength is revealed in our weakness:

"Even to your old age and gray hairs I am he, I am he who will sustain you. I have made you and I will carry you; I will sustain you and I will rescue you" (Isaiah 46:4).

Being 80 years old has also offered me the privilege of cherishing friends and spending more time with my family. It has given me more time to experience God's goodness, love, and faithfulness. **I am genuinely thankful for each day God has given me because it is a gift.** The blessings that God gives me don't stop at a certain age. He provides me with new opportunities daily to serve Him. Your spiritual strength will grow in the church. *"Though outwardly we are wasting away, yet inwardly we are being renewed day by day"* (2 Cor. 4:16). Faith in God will always give you the strength needed to face the world.

Jesus said, **"These things I have spoken to you, that in Me you may have peace. In the world you will have tribulation; but be of good cheer, I have overcome the world"** (John 16:33).

So, what do I want to leave as a legacy for my family? What will they remember most? My first thought is that I hope I leave them with wonderful memories, which can be passed down from generation to generation. I want them to remember that we will meet again in Heaven, so their inheritance is spiritual. I want them to remember that I have been faithful and trusted God until the end.

I remember right before my father passed away, he told me that he wished he had accomplished or done more with his life. In your later years, it is easy to focus on what you didn't do, but look at the many wonderful things you did. Things that at the time seemed so insignificant now seem so special, as you look back and realize that the walk in the park with your wife, the day at the lake with your family, and that camping vacation in the mountains were all very special.

As you age, it is also common to worry about the uncertainty of your future. As people age, their physical abilities, like sight and mobility, decrease and require more assistance with everyday tasks. In many cases, a loss of independence may lead to feelings of frustration or inadequacy. Do you worry about what you would do if an illness occurred or a death in your family?

But Jesus said not to worry about these things: **"Do not let your hearts be troubled. You believe in God; believe also in me. My Father's house has many rooms... I am going there to prepare a place for you"** (John 14:1-3).

> "Do not store up for yourselves treasures on earth, where moths and vermin destroy, and where thieves break in and steal. But store up for yourselves treasures in heaven, where moths and vermin do not destroy, and where thieves do not break in and steal. For where your treasure is, there your heart will be also" (Matthew 16:19-21).

At 80 years old, I love having the pleasure of telling people that my goal is not to make goals anymore. My New Year's Resolution list had nothing on it. Developing a new hobby or skill will help you strengthen your body and brain. ***I read that memory loss is one of the unavoidable parts of growing old. I don't remember what the other items were.***

Growing older and becoming less mobile can undoubtedly cause a decrease in social activities, but don't allow it to get you to the point where feelings of isolation create feelings of depression. I know several folks who are very happy living in one of the friendly retirement living communities.

Losing a little height as you get older is normal. In my dad's latter days, I saw a picture of him and me together and was surprised that he seemed shorter than I remembered. Over the years, the discs between your spine's vertebrae flatten, your muscles start losing mass, and the space between your joints narrows. As a result, people get smaller as they grow older.

God works in every aspect of our lives, including our finances. He guides us and meets our needs. Jesus says, "Ask, using my name, and you will receive, and you will have abundant joy" (John 16:24).

Many people depend more on their credit cards than on Jesus Christ. <u>Before you pay for something, pray for it.</u>

People find that getting old is just plain frustrating. This frustration is compounded with grief if you have lost loved ones and friends. Most injuries to the elderly are the result of falls, so be extra careful in the shower or on the stairs. It's nice to get a call from someone going to the store and ask if you need any groceries or other items. And in today's world, the elderly are becoming more and more vulnerable to scams and different ways to be taken advantage of. Keep a positive but realistic outlook on life and stay as active as possible for as long as possible. ***Don't ever regret growing older; it is a privilege denied to many.***

Old age is not a defeat, but a victory, not a punishment, but a privilege. Walt Disney said, "***Growing old is mandatory, but growing up is optional.***" Mark Twain may have said it best: "***Age is an issue of mind over matter. If you don't mind, it doesn't matter.***"

So, what else do I want to leave as my legacy? I hope my actions can strengthen the faith of others and remind them that God is always faithful. Remember again that you wouldn't be here this long if God were finished with you. He has many more plans for your future. Look ahead confidently and remember that every day is another day to give glory to God.

Interestingly, the Bible contains a command you can obey that will result in a reward of long life. "*Honour thy father and mother; which is the first commandment with promise; that it* may be well with thee, and thou mayest live long on the earth" (Ephesians 6:2–3; Exodus 20:12).

It would seem that, generally speaking, God rewards those who honor their parents with a longer life. Aging is not a lost youth but a new stage of opportunity and strength.

If you believe in Jesus, you have the assurance of an eternity with God. This life we live is but a fleeting moment— Heaven is forever.

A few thoughts to end this subject:

You know you're getting old if you and your teeth don't sleep together.

You try to straighten out the wrinkles in your socks and discover you aren't wearing any.

It takes two or more attempts to get up from the couch.

Your address book has mainly names that start with Doctor.

Everything hurts, and what doesn't hurt doesn't work.

You looked for your glasses for half an hour, and they were on your head the whole time.

You wonder how you could be over the hill when you don't ever remember being on top of it.

Will I See My Baby In Heaven?

I read the story and could only imagine the struggle and anguish that the young woman went through before she decided to have an abortion. This decision was made several years ago, but the thoughts of the child and feelings of guilt may follow her even today. It's not our business to know why she made this decision, but in recent years, she has rededicated her life to Jesus, and her question is – <u>Will I know my baby in heaven?</u> We may never understand the purpose of a child's death, but God assures us that we will see these little ones again.

Abortion: According to the Guttmacher Institute, a research organization that supports access to abortion, more than a million abortions were provided in the U.S. in 2023. Specifically, researchers estimate that there were 1,026,700 abortions in 2023, marking the highest number in over a decade. Guttmacher has conducted this research since 1974.

But abortions are certainly not the only cause of the death of a baby. Birth defects, premature birth, accidents, miscarriages, and other complications are also involved. Sources vary, but many estimate that approximately 1 in 4 pregnancies end in miscarriage. Regardless of the reason, nothing can be more agonizing than the death of a child.

Abortion as we know it today was not practiced in biblical times, but it is clear from the scriptures that **an unborn baby is known by the Lord, even from the time of conception**.

> *"For thou hast possessed my reins: thou hast covered me in my mother's womb. I will praise thee; for I am fearfully and wonderfully made: marvellous are thy works; and that my soul knoweth right well. My substance was not hid from thee, when I was made in secret, and curiously wrought in the lowest parts of the earth. Thine eyes did see my substance, yet being unperfect; and in thy book all my members were written, which in continuance were fashioned, when as yet there was none of them"* (Psalms 139:13–16).

I read somewhere, "You are no less a mom than the pregnant women you see around you. Your motherhood is still valid and beautiful. You carried a life inside you, for however long, and you'll carry your love and loss for your child forever."

So, where are the Babies that are never born because of Miscarriages or Abortions? What about that child that you have never met? According to the scripture, you will see and know that baby. That child is a person from the moment of conception, and when death occurred, the child was taken by the Father to heaven. They did not have a chance to understand the gospel and salvation. All the threats of Hell in the Bible are reserved for those who have sinned knowingly and willingly.

I genuinely believe that one day in the future, God will allow you to hold that child in your arms. *"It is not the will of your Father in heaven that one of these little ones should perish."* Scripture indicates God's great love for those who die in the womb, and this gives credence to the belief that God takes the souls of aborted children to heaven with Him.

Concerning the statement *"all unborn babies go to heaven."* Some people might think there is nothing wrong with abortion. Wouldn't an abortion guarantee the innocent unborn child a place in God's eternal kingdom? This is false reasoning. Apply this same argument to little children who have not yet reached the age of accountability. Should we, like King Herod, round up all the two-year-olds and put them to death? Wouldn't we be sending them straight to paradise? The answer is obviously NO!

Innocent Babies/Children: The Bible teaches us that *"the wages of sin is death."* (Romans 6:23). Neither an unborn child nor an aborted baby has had the opportunity to sin willfully. However, every child conceived bears the sin naturally inherited from Adam and is therefore subject to judgment. At the same time, God, in His grace and mercy, can apply the sacrifice of Christ to the unborn victims of abortion. We know Christ's blood is sufficient for such a thing because Jesus died *"for the sins of the whole world."* (1 John 2:2). Children are not responsible in the same way as those whose sins are willful and premeditated. That is why He refers to them as "innocents." Jeremiah 2:34 says, *"Also on your skirts is found the blood of the lives of the poor innocents."*

God is given the name "**Father**," and that alone should tell you about His character. *"But You, O Lord, are a God full of compassion, and gracious, longsuffering and abundant in mercy and truth"* (Psalms 86:15).

A Reunion in Heaven: In 2 Samuel chapter 12, King David was confronted by the prophet Nathan after he had committed adultery with Bathsheba and had Bathsheba's husband, Uriah the Hittite, killed. God told Nathan to go and tell David that the child he and Bathsheba had brought into the world would be taken away in death. On the day that the child became ill and died, David washed and anointed himself, changed clothes, and went into the house of the Lord and worshiped. His servants asked him why he had fasted and wept for the child while he was alive, but when the child died, he arose and ate food.

David's response was, *"While the child was alive, I fasted and wept; for I said, 'Who can tell whether the Lord will be gracious to me, that the child may live?' But now he is dead; why should I fast? Can I bring him back again? <u>I shall go to him, but he shall not return to me</u>."* The thought of a reunion with his child cheered David on, and that reunion would happen in heaven. Babies have not had a chance to know our Creator, so the grace and mercy of God intercede on their behalf.

Jesus and the Children: Little children were brought to Him that He might put His hands on them and pray, but the disciples rebuked them. But Jesus said, *"Let the little children come to Me, and do not forbid them; for of such is the kingdom of heaven."* The term "little children" could also mean "little babies."

The disciples also came to Jesus, saying, *"Who then is greatest in the kingdom of heaven?"* Then Jesus called a little child to Him, and set him in the midst of them, and said:

"Assuredly, I say to you, unless you are converted and become as little children, you will by no means enter the kingdom of heaven. Therefore whoever humbles himself as this little child is the greatest in the kingdom of heaven. Whoever receives a little child like this in My name receives Me" (Matthew 19:13-14). Jesus repeatedly demonstrated His compassion and his incredible love for little children.

God's Children: God considers all children His: "Moreover, *you took your sons and your daughters, whom you bore to Me."* God is not going to do anything unrighteous with his children.

Israel's people were denied entrance into the Promised Land because they didn't believe in God's help. But the scripture states the children were exempted from that penalty: **"*Moreover your little ones and your children, who you say will be victims, who today have no knowledge of good and evil, they shall go in there; to them I will give it, and they shall possess it"*** (Deuteronomy 1:39). God did not hold the children responsible for the unbelief of the adults.

Age of Accountability: This is when children can understand God's love and what it means to be a sinner. The blood of Jesus covers these children until they can understand good vs. evil, and then they become responsible. For some children, that knowledge comes at a very early age, and it may take more time for some. It is a reckoning of spiritual understanding.

We often see the age of accountability in action when a child attends Sunday school or on a Vacation Bible School trip. Someone will present the gospel, and they know that they need to be saved. Little children have no record of unbelief or evil works, and therefore, there is no basis for their deserving an eternity apart from God.

When should a child be baptized? God does not expect the impossible, so why should He expect an unborn child to be baptized? He doesn't. These innocent children are precisely that, innocent. While they have not had the opportunity to receive baptism, they also have not had the opportunity to accept or reject God. He will not reject them.

Baptism should only occur when they understand the gospel and share why they want to be a Christian. Then they can be baptized. But remember that there is no guarantee that when a child reaches the age of accountability, they will automatically want to follow Jesus.

How old are these Children going to be in Heaven? There is no absolute answer in the Scripture, but some believe that when we are in heaven, we will all be mature in body, mind, and spirit. Some believe that children will be allowed to grow up in Heaven. Keep in mind that there are children in the future kingdom of Jesus, *"And the sucking child shall play on the hole of the asp, and the weaned child shall put his hand on the cockatrice' den. They shall not hurt nor destroy in all my holy mountain: for the earth shall be full of the knowledge of the LORD"* (Isaiah 11:8-9).

One theory is that babies are given a resurrection body that is "fast-forwarded" to the "ideal age." Likewise, those who die at an old age are "re-wound" to the ideal age. Some believe this perfect age to be around 30. Some say 33 since that is approximately the age Jesus was when He died. This ideal age concept is not specifically biblical. But one thing is certain, whatever age we appear to be, we will be gloriously perfect.

I read a comment from teacher J. Vernon McGee in which he stated:

> *"I believe with all my heart that God will raise the little ones such that the mother's arms who have ached for them will have the opportunity of holding them. The father's hand, which never held the little hand will be given the privilege. I believe that little ones will grow up in heaven in the care of their earthly parents if they are saved."*

Moment of Conception: Every individual ever conceived is created "in the Image of God" (Genesis 1:27). The Bible clearly indicates that God knows and regards us as unique human persons even while we are still in the womb (and even before that time).

We started with this question, so let's end with it: "Will I know my baby in Heaven?" There is no question that God will take your baby to Heaven, but as Dr. David Jeremiah once stated, the question is, *"Will you be there with them? To enjoy this heavenly reunion, you must come to know Jesus Christ."*

Coming Home

(A prayer dedicated to Virgil Wilson, my fishing buddy now in heaven)

As I look back on my life, dear Lord
The gifts I received are beyond measure
And I realize that my faith, family, and friends
They are truly my greatest treasure

I now seem to worry less
About all of life's constant strife
Because, dear Lord, you've given me
The promise of eternal life

Life certainly has its ups and downs
But you held my hand through it all
And with your support and direction, my Lord
I knew I would never fall

Thank you, Lord, for allowing me
A wonderful life and so much more
You gave me a fresh start every day
So that I could be a better person than the day before

But as in all things the Bible states
Our life here on earth will end
And as Christians we will be carried away
To a place that has no sin

My salvation comes from believing, Lord
In Jesus Christ your Son
And if death is an end to pain and suffering
Then this earthly battle will be won

My request, dear Lord, is to come take me home
Take my tired and anguished body I pray
My thoughts are to be with my heavenly friends
And if it be your will, O Lord, let it happen this way

As a person I certainly fear dying
But as a Christian death will set me free
And seeing my Lord's heavenly face
Will mean everything to me

My prayer is that my family's grief
Will be softened somewhat by the thought
That we will all meet once again in Heaven
This is God's promise that we have all been taught

An eternity with God in His heavenly home
A time with no sin, pain, or sorrow
It's exciting for this believer to think
That I might see my God tomorrow

My Lord, my God, my Heavenly King
I so look forward to the day
When your angels will escort me to Heaven
Where for eternity I will stay

The heavenly gates will open wide
The angels will welcome me
But most of all I will finally see
Jesus Christ who set me free

I am at peace Lord and my soul is now at rest
My comfort is in your Word, Lord, and I am truly blessed
My last breath on earth really gives me little stress
For I know my next moment in Heaven will be my very best

The Seven Spirits of God

The "seven spirits of God" are mentioned four times in the Book of Revelation. The "seven spirits" are recognized as the Holy Spirit, and "seven" refers to perfection and completion. John was talking to the seven churches in the province of Asia (Revelation 1:4-5).

> *"Grace and peace to you from him who is, and who was, and who is to come, and from <u>the seven spirits</u> before his throne. And from Jesus Christ, who is the faithful witness, and the first begotten of the dead, and the prince of the kings of the earth. Unto him that loved us, and washed us from our sins in his own blood."*

This is a part of John's greeting to the seven churches in Asia, in which he invokes the grace and peace of the triune God. The Asia spoken of here is the Roman province of Asia, which was in modern-day Turkey. The capital of the Roman province of Asia was *Pergamos*, which was also the home of one of the seven churches. John appears to be listing the members of the Trinity, and it seems he is describing a <u>manifestation of the Holy Spirit as the seven spirits of God</u>.

Jesus also says He "has" the seven spirits and stated that He would send the Holy Spirit as a Helper after He ascended. The help given by the Holy Spirit would be better for the disciples than if Jesus remained on the earth at that time (John 16:7).

> *"And to the angel of the church in Sardis write, 'These things says He who has the seven Spirits of God and the seven stars: "I know your works, that you have a name that you are alive, but you are dead."*

Jesus issues a message to the church in Sardis, warning them to awaken from spiritual deadness and renew their faithfulness to God in order to receive His approval and avoid judgment. He identifies himself to the church as having the <u>seven Spirits of God</u> (the Holy Spirit) <u>and the seven stars</u>, a reference to the messengers or pastors of the seven churches.

> ***"From the throne came flashes of lightning, rumblings and peals of thunder. In front of the throne, seven lamps were blazing. These are the seven spirits of God"*** (Revelation 4:5).

John sees God on his throne, and God is worshipped unceasingly. Some view the lightning, thundering, and voices that proceed from the throne as indications of approaching judgments, but others view them as tokens of God's power of judgment. The seven Spirits of God are symbolized as seven burning lamps before God's throne. This compares with Zechariah's vision:

> *"And said unto me, What seest thou? And I said, I have looked, and behold a candlestick all of gold, with a bowl upon the top of it, and his seven lamps thereon, and seven pipes to the seven lamps, which are upon the top thereof"* (Zechariah 4:2).

John describes how he saw Jesus as a Lamb standing at God's throne, circled by four living creatures, angelic beings or cherubim representing all of creation. The elders represent the complete body of the redeemed, combining Old Testament saints (12 tribes) and New Testament believers (12 apostles). This interpretation reflects the unity of God's people across history (Matthew 19:28; Revelation 21:12-14).

> *"Then I saw a Lamb, looking as if it had been slain, standing at the center of the throne, encircled by the four living creatures and the elders. The Lamb had seven horns and seven eyes, which are the seven spirits of God sent out into all the earth"* (Revelation 5:6).

The living creatures are reminiscent of the cherubim described in Ezekiel 1 and the seraphim in Isaiah 6 that serve as guardians of God's holiness and as perpetual worshipers.

The Lamb had seven horns and seven eyes. Horns are a scriptural metaphor for divine power, and <u>the seven eyes are the seven Spirits</u> sent out into all the earth (omnipresence).

So, if the "seven Spirits" are identified as the Holy Spirit, why are there seven of them?

The Bible uses the number seven to refer to perfection and completion. John's vision includes a picture of the perfect and complete Holy Spirit. This verse references the Holy Spirit with a seven-fold description (Isaiah 11:2).

> *"And the spirit of the Lord shall rest upon him, the spirit of wisdom and understanding, the spirit of counsel and might, the spirit of knowledge and of the fear of the Lord."*

The "Spirit of the Lord" is interpreted as the third Person of the Trinity. The Holy Spirit is one person, but empowered with seven key ministries:

1. The Spirit of the LORD
2. The Spirit of Wisdom
3. The Spirit of Understanding
4. The Spirit of Counsel
5. The Spirit of Power
6. The Spirit of Knowledge
7. The Spirit of the Fear of the Lord

We can cultivate the seven gifts of the Spirit by staying connected to God through prayer, meditation, and studying scripture. As we develop a deeper relationship with God, the Spirit will help us seek wisdom and understanding, which will allow us to make better decisions and overcome challenges. The fear of the Lord will give us great respect and reverence for His authority. The seven gifts of the Spirit will allow us to strengthen our Christian life.

The prophecy is that the Messiah would be empowered not by seven individual spirits but by the One Spirit, described in seven ways.

The "seven spirits of God" refer to the Holy Spirit in the fullness of His manifold ministry.

"The Spirit itself beareth witness with our spirit, that we are the children of God" (Romans 8:16).

What Does the Number 40 Mean in the Bible?

It's strange, but I never noticed this before. According to an internet search, the English word "forty" or the number "40" appears 158 times in 145 King James Bible verses. This breaks down to 134 occurrences in the Old Testament and 24 times in the New Testament. Most scholars believe that when you see the term "forty days" in Scripture, it literally means "forty days." I guess the question is, did God choose this number to have a special meaning? Here are a few scriptures that mention forty:

God had **Noah** build an ark, and then God sent rain on the earth for <u>forty days and forty nights</u>, and every living thing except those on the ark were killed (Genesis 7:4–17). ***Isaac*** was the son of Abraham and the father of Jacob. He was <u>forty</u>

years old when he married Rebekah (Genesis 25:20). Forty days were required for embalming (Genesis 50:3).

Moses spent 40 years in Egypt as a prince, 40 years as a shepherd, and 40 years in the wilderness. God was grooming him for his future role of leading Israel out of Egypt's bondage (Acts 7; Numbers 14:34).

God tells **Moses** to choose a leader from each of the 12 tribes to go into the land of Canaan and bring back a report, along with some of the fruit of the land. The men spent 40 days exploring the land, and when they came back, they relayed that God was right about the bounty and beauty of the land, but they feared the strength and size of the inhabitants of the land. Only Caleb and Joshua trusted the Lord. God told the Israelites that they would wander in the desert for **one year for every day the spies were in the land—a total of 40 years**. Everyone above 20 years of age, except faithful Joshua and Caleb, would die during that time. **Moses** was on Mount Sinai for 40 days and nights, on two separate occasions, receiving God's laws (Exodus 24:18).

> *"For the Lord your God has blessed you in all the works of your hand. He knows your trudging through this great wilderness. These forty years the Lord your God has been with you; you have lacked nothing"* (Deuteronomy 2:7).

The **Israelites** had to spend 40 years wandering in the wilderness. They kept looking back toward Egypt whenever they ran into the slightest trial. Their shoes did not fall apart or need to be replaced over 40 years (Deuteronomy 8:25; 9:18; 25).

40 lashes (stripes) were the maximum whipping penalty (Deuteronomy 25:3). **God allowed the land to rest** for 40 years (Judges 3:11; 5:31; 8:28). **Abdon**, a judge in Israel, had 40 sons (Judges 12:14). And the people of **Israel** again did what was evil in the sight of the Lord, so the Lord gave them into the hand of the Philistines for forty years (Judges 13:1).

Eli fell backward from his seat by the side of the gate, breaking his neck and causing his death, for the man was old and heavy. He had judged Israel for forty years (1 Samuel 4:18). In the story of the giant **Goliath**, the Philistine and Israelite armies stood on opposite sides for 40 days, and each day, Goliath taunted the Israelite army. After 40 days, **God sent David** to defeat the giant and the Philistines (1 Samuel 17:16).

David was thirty years old when he began to reign. He reigned for forty years (2 Samuel 5:4). **Solomon** reigned in Jerusalem over all Israel for forty years (1 Kings 11:42). The holy place of the temple was 40 cubits long (1 Kings 6:17). They asked for a king, and God gave them **Saul** the son of Kish, a man of the tribe of Benjamin, for forty years (Acts 13:21).

Ishbosheth (Saul's son) was 40 years old when he began to reign (2 Samuel 2:10). ***Joash*** reigned 40 years in Jerusalem (2 Kings 12:1). And he (***Elijah***) arose and ate and drank, and went in the strength of that food forty days and forty nights to Horeb, the mount of God (1 Kings 19:8).

And when you (**Ezekiel**) have completed these, you shall lie down a second time, but on your right side, and bear the punishment of the house of Judah. I assign you forty days, a day for each year (Ezekiel 4:6; 29:13).

Then Jesus was led up by the Spirit into the wilderness to be tempted by the devil. After fasting for forty days and forty nights, he was hungry. The tempter said to him, "If you are the Son of God, command these stones to become loaves of bread." But he answered, "It is written, 'Man shall not live by bread alone, but by every word that comes from the mouth of God'" (Matthew 4:1-25; Mark 1:13; and Luke 4:1-2). And after his crucifixion and resurrection, ***Jesus*** remained and walked with His disciples for 40 days and nights before ascending to heaven (Acts 1:3).

WOW!! The number forty seems to have a special meaning in the Bible because it is linked with many scriptures. We see it used in periods of testing and judgment, divine intervention and revelation, renewal and transformation, completion and fulfillment, repentance and forgiveness, and in leadership and authority. Most of these scriptures mark periods when God prepares people for a new spiritual journey and growth phase.

Whether forty has any significance is still being debated, and the Bible does not explicitly assign any special meaning to it. But the number is sure to be used a lot.

God Balances the Universe

God rules and controls all things. So, how does God create, maintain, manage, and balance everything? Mankind certainly can't balance much, because many of us have trouble balancing our checkbook.

Let's start this study with "***Who created God?***" According to the Bible, nobody created God. He is by nature the eternal God, who always was, is, and always will be. He has no beginning and will have no end. God is self-existent and uncreated. God is understood as the supreme being and the creator of the universe. God initiated the existence of the world through deliberate and purposeful creation. God brought the universe without pre-existing materials, emphasizing His absolute power and sovereignty over all creation.

The concept of the ***Trinity*** asserts that **one God is existing eternally in three distinct persons: Father, Son (Jesus Christ), and Holy Spirit.** God continues to sustain and uphold the universe. The Apostle Paul writes, "*In Him, all things hold together*" (Colossians 1:17), emphasizing God's ongoing role in maintaining order and existence. The act of creation manifests God's glory and creative wisdom. "*The heavens declare the glory of God; the skies proclaim the work of His hands*" (Psalms 19:1).

God's nature is characterized by His ***Omnipotence*** (all-powerful), ***Omniscience*** (all-knowing), ***Omnipresence*** (present everywhere), and ***Omnibenevolence*** (perfectly good and loving).

The Book of Genesis states, **"In the beginning, God created the heavens and the earth."** God's creative act brought forth the universe and all living things. Scripture teaches us that God created the world and everything in it for His glory and desires to share His time with others.

God created the Heavens and the Earth as follows:

> Day 1: God created light and separated it from darkness,
> Day 2: God made the firmament to divide the waters,
> Day 3: Dry land appeared, along with vegetation,
> Day 4: God created the sun, moon, and stars.
> Day 5: Birds and sea creatures came into existence,
> Day 6: Land animals and humans were formed,
> Day 7: God rested (Genesis 1:1–31).

So, what was God doing before He created the world? This answer to this question cannot be fully understood from a human perspective. Humans process life as a timeline; one day/week/month/year after another, and we can only exist in the present. But God created time, and He exists in a dimension not bound by time. He sees and interacts in the past, present, and future concurrently. You can't measure "before" without the concept of time.

How old is our planet? Scientists analyzing light and other types of radiation believe it is about 13.8 billion years old. They continue to refine the answer as telescope technology improves. However, a strictly literal approach to the book of Genesis puts the universe at around **6,000 years old**. Taking the creation account in Genesis 1 to refer to 24-hour days and calculating back from the genealogies in Genesis 5 and 11, Adam would have been created around 4000 BC. The Earth would have been created just days prior, so assuming the entire universe was made at the same time, it, too, would be about 6,000 years old.

Some people have different opinions on the interpretation of the word "**day**" (Hebrew "*yom*"). Those who hold to a literal, 24-hour day believe in a comparatively young earth; those who hold to a non-literal, poetic day believe in a much older world. Some views are more biblical than others, and a person's specific viewpoint is based on their faith in the evidence presented.

The "**Big Bang**" is a theory developed during the twentieth century that tries to describe how the universe expanded from a primordial state of nothing but high density and temperature. Atheism particularly holds to the idea of an "infinitely old" universe as a reason to dismiss God as unnecessary. Over several decades, those who preferred the idea of an eternal universe made many attempts to explain away hard evidence, but to no avail. The result was secular science that gives tremendous support to the creation account in the Bible.

The work of Edwin Hubble in the 1920s states that the universe is expanding, which requires a beginning. If the universe is currently expanding, then at some time in the past, the entire universe would have been contained in some infinitesimally small point. This idea is foundational to the Big Bang theory and is an example of misguided science and theology.

According to objective, empirical science, all space, time, and energetic particles came into existence together in a single moment: a "beginning." Before this event, whatever it was, there was no time and no space. Then, suddenly, an exceedingly dense, incredibly hot, infinitesimal ball of something—everything appeared somewhere, somehow, for reasons unknown, and began to expand rapidly with our whole universe inside of it. These energy particles spread out, cooled, and formed neutral hydrogen gas. The big question is – where did these energy particles, gases, and space come from to create the Big Bang? <u>The story ends like a bad dream</u>.

It is hard to dispute that God created every living thing in this cosmos and on Earth. Many Christians have come to feel that the Big Bang theory attempts to undermine the biblical account of creation. That said, it is important to understand that the Big Bang theory is just that – a theory.

"By faith we understand that the universe was formed at God's command, so that what is seen was not made out of what was visible" (Hebrews 11:3).

"By the word of the Lord the heavens were made, their starry host by the breath of his mouth" (Psalms 33:6).

So, how big is this universe that God created? It's estimated to be 93 billion light-years in diameter, and one light-year is equivalent to 6 trillion miles. Remember, that's not the end of the universe – only the part we can see with our advanced technology. The universe might be 250 times larger than the part we see, which would be at least 7 trillion light-years in diameter.

Based on the data available, the current best guess is that there are between 5 and 10 billion potentially habitable planets in our galaxy. This was the conclusion reached by a team of researchers at Penn State University in August 2019. They examined numerous factors such as size, orbital times, and distance to the nearest star of planets discovered so far, and extrapolated from that. This is a huge number, but bear in mind that there are thought to be around 400 billion planets in the Milky Way in total. Therefore, we estimate that between 1% and 2.5% of the planets in our galaxy are habitable. There are estimated to be around 21.6 sextillion (21,600,000,000,000,000,000,000) planets in our observable universe.

The most powerful telescopes on Earth and in space can see objects billions of light-years away, such as galaxies and quasars. The Hubble Space Telescope, for example, has observed galaxies that are more than 13 billion light-years away. Without a telescope, we can see about 6,000 stars in the sky. That may seem like many stars, but for every star you can see, there are probably more than 20 million you cannot see.

The **Milky Way** is a massive collection of stars, dust, and gas. It's called a spiral galaxy because viewing it from the top or bottom would look like a spinning pinwheel. The Sun is located on one of the spiral arms, about 25,000 light-years from the galaxy's center. Even if you could travel at the speed of light (186,000 miles per second), it would take you about 25,000 years to reach the middle of the Milky Way.

The Milky Way name comes from a Greek myth about the goddess **Hera,** who sprayed milk across the sky. In other parts of the world, our galaxy goes by different names. In China, it's called the *"Silver River,"* and in the Kalahari Desert in Southern Africa, it's called the *"Backbone of Night."* Scientists estimate that the Milky Way contains between 100 and 400 billion stars (though some think there could be as many as a trillion).

Our planetary system is called the **Solar System**, referring to the name of our Sun and eight planets. The eight planets in our Solar System, in order from the Sun, are the four terrestrial planets Mercury, Venus, Earth, and Mars, followed by the two gas giants Jupiter and Saturn, the ice giants Uranus and Neptune, and the dwarf planet Pluto.

The smallest planet in our Solar System is Mercury, which is only one-third the size of Earth, while the biggest planet in the Solar System is Jupiter, which is 11 times bigger than Earth. More than 1,300 Earths could fit inside Jupiter if it were hollow. It would take about seven months to get to Mars (the closest planet to us), 15 months to reach Venus, six years to reach Jupiter, seven years to reach Saturn, 8.5 years to reach Uranus, 9.5 years to reach Pluto, and twelve years to get to Neptune.

Our **Sun** has a radius of about 435,000 miles, roughly 109 times the diameter of the Earth, and about 1.3 million Earths could fit inside it. Without the Sun, photosynthesis would stop, most plants would die, and any humans left on the planet's surface would see frigid and dangerous conditions.

The **Moon** is about 236,121 miles from the Earth, and its diameter is more than a quarter of the Earth's. Without a Moon, there would be dark skies every night, and there would be no eclipses. The Tides would also be significantly affected. Earth spins on its axis, tilted at 23.4° to our orbital plane around the Sun. Without a Moon, our tilt might exceed 45° at times, making us a world that spins on its side. Poles wouldn't always be cold, and the equator might not be warm.

The **Earth's** average orbital speed is about 29.8 kilometers per second (66,660 mph). This is precisely the speed it needs to be going to counteract the force of gravity from the sun pulling it inward. Without the outward centripetal force to counteract the inward pull of gravity, it would take about 65 days for the Earth to plunge into the Sun.

Our Earth comprises three layers: the **Crust**, the **Mantle**, and the **Core**. The crust is the outside layer and is made of solid rock, mostly basalt and granite.

The *mantle* lies below the crust and consists of hot, dense, iron—and magnesium-rich solid rock. The crust and the upper part of the mantle make up the lithosphere, which is broken into large and small plates. The *core* is the center of the Earth and comprises a liquid outer core and a solid inner core. The outer core is made of nickel, iron, and molten rock. Temperatures here can reach up to 50,000 °C. The pressure in the Earth's core is more than 3,000 times greater than at the bottom of our deepest ocean. A tunnelling machine would be crushed and cooked long before reaching the Earth's core.

The Earth's core ranges from about 8,000 to 10,800 degrees Fahrenheit. The sun's core is a staggering 27 million degrees Fahrenheit, and the surface has a temperature of about 5,500 degrees Fahrenheit. Lightning can heat the air it passes through to 50,000 degrees Fahrenheit, about 5 times hotter than the sun's surface. When lightning strikes a tree, the heat vaporizes any water in its path, possibly causing the tree to explode or a strip of bark to be blown off.

 The **tilt of Earth's axis** is the leading cause of the seasons. If Earth had no tilt, then the length of daylight and the intensity of solar heating seen by a person standing at a single place on the surface would be the same all year round. If the Earth were one inch closer to the Sun, the warming would cause glaciers to melt, sea levels would rise, and there would be much flooding.

God is a master of balancing all things. If this balance were destroyed, mankind's environment and existence would be destroyed. God created areas in the world covered with ice and snow year-round, while the four seasons are like summer in other places. Some mountains are covered in lush vegetation, but there is not even a single blade of grass growing in another range of mountains. God uses various methods to balance our world and the living conditions for mankind, all kinds of plants, animals, birds, and insects. God's goal was to allow all living beings to live and multiply under His established laws. Everything that God does is for a reason and fits His majestic plan.

Covenants in the Bible

The Bible isn't a random collection of stories and moral principles; it's a story about Jesus and God's kingdom. As the stories in the Bible unfold, it becomes apparent that the covenants God makes with his people are extremely important. The word "**covenant**" in the Bible comes from the Hebrew "*běriyth*" and the Greek word "*diatheke*." These words have slightly different meanings but are translated as "covenant."

In the Bible, there are at least eight covenants between God and His people that state specific promises and sanctions that will occur. Although theologians differ over the precise number and nature of such divine covenants, the word covenant doesn't need to be present if the elements of a covenant relationship are present. Learning about covenants will give us a better understanding of our commitment to God as believers.

Conditional covenants are based on certain obligations and prerequisites; the covenant is broken if the requirements are not fulfilled.

Unconditional covenants are made with no strings attached and will be kept regardless of one party's fidelity or infidelity. God promises to fulfill these irrespective of other factors.

General covenants are not specific to one people group and can involve a wide range of people.

The Adamic Covenant was <u>unconditional</u> and can be thought of in two parts: the ***Edenic Covenant*** (works) and the ***Adamic Covenant*** (Grace).

    1. The Edenic Covenant: This establishes God's rule and relationship with mankind (Genesis 1:26-30; 2:16-17). The details of this covenant include the following: Mankind (male and female) is created in God's image, Mankind has dominion (rule) over the animal kingdom, mankind is divinely directed to reproduce and inhabit the entire Earth, and Mankind is to be vegetarians. Eating the fruit of the Tree of the Knowledge of Good and Evil is forbidden, with death as the stated penalty.

    2. The Adamic Covenant: This was initiated because of Adam's sin (Genesis 3:16-19). The following curses were pronounced: Enmity between Satan and Eve and her descendants, Painful childbirth for women, Marital strife, Soil cursed, Thorns and thistles introduced, Survival to be a struggle, Death was introduced, and Death would be the inescapable fate of all living things.

    Although these curses are severe and inescapable, a tremendous promise of grace was also included in the Adamic

Covenant (Genesis 3:15) and is often referred to as the "Proto-Gospel" or "First Gospel." God promises that one born of a woman would be wounded in the process of destroying Satan. The "seed" of the woman who would crush the Serpent's head is Jesus Christ (Galatians 4:4). Even during the curse, God's gracious provision of salvation shines through.

3. The Noahic Covenant: This reinstates God's authority over man and man's responsibilities as stated in the Adamic Covenant and adds new responsibilities such as the relationship of man and the animal kingdom, eating animal flesh, draining of blood before eating meat, establishing the death penalty, and being fruitful and multiplying on the earth (Gen 8:20; 9:3-18). God made this covenant with Noah and his sons after the flood waters receded and everyone left the Ark.

The Bible says that God caused a rainbow to appear in the sky on that day and used it to promise Noah and all of mankind that He would never again destroy the earth and all its inhabitants in a worldwide flood. Neither mankind's wickedness nor righteousness affects this <u>unconditional</u> covenant.

This does not mean that God will never again destroy the earth, because He has promised to one day destroy the world by fire (2 Peter 3:10). The lesson is that when we see a rainbow, we should constantly be reminded of God's faithfulness and His amazing grace. God *"is patient toward you, not wishing that any should perish, but that all should reach repentance"* (2 Pet. 2:9).

4. The Abrahamic Covenant: The story of Israel begins in the book of Genesis when God makes a binding covenant with Abraham, who was to become the father of the Jewish nation. This covenant consisted of four <u>unconditional</u> promises that consisted of: (1) God's promise to bless Abraham, (2) Out of Abraham will come a great nation, (3) Abraham will be a blessing to many and, (4) God will bless those who bless Israel and curse those who curse her.

God changed Abram's name from Abram ("high father") to Abraham ("father of a multitude"). The covenant mentions "making Israel a great nation", but the ultimate greatness will occur during the Millennium. God also gave Abraham the rite of circumcision as the specific sign of the Abrahamic Covenant (Genesis 17:9-14). This covenant also promised that the number of Abraham's children would rival that of "the dust of the earth" (Genesis 15:16-17), and that nations and kings would proceed from him.

The Abrahamic Covenant also included a promise of blessing and redemption (Genesis 12:3). All the earth would be blessed through Abraham. God fulfilled his promise to Abraham by sending his only begotten Son, Jesus, to the earth as the Savior of the world to be born in the flesh from a descendant of Abraham.

All who receive Christ as Savior are the true heirs of Abraham and have all rights and privileges. Abraham believed God would keep his promise, "*and if you are Christ's, then you are Abraham's offspring, heirs according to promise*" (Galatians 3:29). And of utmost importance with this covenant is the restoration of the Jewish people to their land. The promises made by God are far-reaching and eternal. I read once that – History states that Israel stands at the graves of all its enemies. It is something to think about.

5. Mosaic Covenant: This is a <u>conditional</u> covenant made between God and the nation of Israel and completed through the ministry of Jesus Christ (Exodus 19-24). It is sometimes called the Sinai Covenant since God gave His divine law to Moses on Mount Sinai. God reminded the people of their obligation to obey His law, and they agreed to the covenant when they said, "*All that the Lord has spoken we will do!*"

This covenant would set the nation of Israel apart from all other nations as God's chosen people. God would also sovereignly decide to bless the world with His written Word and His Living Word, Jesus Christ. The blessings and curses associated with this conditional covenant are found in Deuteronomy 28.

The Mosaic Law would reveal to people their sinfulness and their need for a Savior, and it is the Mosaic Law that Christ Himself said that He did not come to abolish but to fulfill. This covenant was extremely important for two reasons: (1) It showed the nation of Israel (and us) the impossibility of keeping God's law perfectly, and (2) It provided a forum for Christ to come and be the perfect Son of Israel and serve as the ultimate sacrifice for all sin.

The Mosaic covenant also stated that sacrificial worship was how Yahweh and Israel's divine-human relationship could be maintained. This covenant shows us that, because of indwelling sin, the Law is something that mankind can never appease (Romans 3:19-20). Yet, through faith in Christ, we are declared righteous before God.

6. The Davidic Covenant: This is <u>unconditional</u> and refers to God's promises to David through Nathan the prophet (2 Samuel 7), and later summarized in 1 Chronicles 17:11-14 and 2 Chronicles 6:16. This covenant lays the foundation by which the future Millennial kingdom will be established. God promises David and Israel that the Messiah (Jesus Christ) would come from the lineage of David and the tribe of Judah, and He would establish a kingdom that would endure forever. The surety of the promises made rests solely on God's faithfulness and does not depend at all on David or Israel's obedience. The Davidic Covenant also reaffirmed the promise of the land that God made in the first two covenants with Israel (the Abrahamic and Mosaic Covenants).

> *"I will provide a place for my people Israel and will plant them so that they can have a home of their own and no longer be disturbed. Wicked people will not oppress them anymore"* (2 Samuel 7:10).

God then promises that David's son will succeed him as king of Israel and that his son (Solomon) will build the temple (2 Samuel 7:12-13). Overall, this was the promise of an everlasting kingdom.

It is written that another Son of David, the Messiah Jesus Christ, will rule forever and build a lasting House.

"Your house and your kingdom will endure forever before me; your throne will be established forever" (2 Samuel 7:16).

Other references to the Davidic Covenant are in Jeremiah 23:5; 30:9; Isaiah 9:7; 11:1; and Luke 1:32.

Many OT prophesies and promises will be fulfilled during the 1000-year Millennium reign of Christ. *"He will be great and will be called the Son of the Most High. The Lord God will give him the throne of his father David, and he will reign over Jacob's descendants forever; his kingdom will never end"* (Luke 1:32-33). Unlike mere human rulers who disappoint us with their failure to rule justly, Jesus obeyed God in all things, even giving his own life out of his love for the world. He earned the right to rule in glory forever (John 3:16; 1 Kings 2:35; Revelation 11:15).

The resurrected Christ is the one truly righteous King who has secured eternal life for all believers and will end all injustice and evil one day (Revelation 21:4).

7. Land Covenant: This is sometimes called the Palestinian Covenant (Deuteronomy 29:1-29; 30:1-10). It was made between God and Israel right before Moses died and Israel entered the Promised Land. This unconditional covenant basically relates to Israel's possession of the entire territory promised to them—present-day Israel, Lebanon, the West Bank of Jordan, and portions of Syria, Iraq, and Saudi Arabia.

On a future day, the Messiah will return to set up His righteous rule, and the world will be blessed with peace, pleasure, and prosperity. God made this covenant with Israel after the Mosaic Covenant and after Israel had wandered in the wilderness for forty years. The covenant would remind the new generation of Israelites of their relationship with the almighty God.

This covenant has many similarities to the Mosaic Covenant but is a separate and distinct covenant as clearly seen in (Deuteronomy 29:1): *"These are the words of the covenant which the Lord commanded Moses to make with the children of Israel in the land of Moab, besides the covenant which He made with them in Horeb."*

Before making this covenant with Israel, God reminded them that if they obeyed the Mosaic Law, He would bless the nation abundantly and warned them that disobedience to the Law would result in His cursing the country (Deuteronomy 28:1-68). This covenant also contains some special promises to Israel that many believe will not be completely fulfilled until the Millennial reign of Christ, such as:

- Gathering the scattered Israelites from all over the world and bringing them back into the land He had promised to their ancestors,
- Regenerating the Israelites by circumcising their hearts so that they would love Him totally,
- Judging Israel's enemies,
- And if Israel would obey God, He would prosper them for their obedience (Deuteronomy 30:3-9). Someday, the seed of Abraham will possess the Promised Land forever.

8. The New Covenant: This covenant provides for the future spiritual regeneration during the Millennial kingdom (Jeremiah 31:31-37). God promises all of humanity that He will forgive sin and restore fellowship with those whose hearts are turned toward Him. According to the NT Gospels and letters, the New Covenant was ratified through Jesus's death on the cross.

This covenant was predicted while the Old Covenant was still in effect by the prophets Moses, Jeremiah, and Ezekiel. The

Old Covenant that God had established with His people required strict obedience to the Mosaic Law, and the Law required that Israel perform daily sacrifices to atone for sin. But Moses, through whom God established the Old Covenant, also anticipated the New Covenant. In one of his final addresses to the nation of Israel, Moses looked forward to a time when Israel would be given *"a heart to understand."*

Moses predicted that Israel would fail to keep the Old Covenant, but he saw a restoration time. At that time, Moses said, *"The Lord your God will circumcise your hearts and the hearts of your descendants, so that you may love him with all your heart and with all your soul, and live."*

The New Covenant involves a total change of heart so that God's people are naturally pleasing to Him. Jesus Christ came to fulfill the Law of Moses (Matthew 5:17) and to establish the New Covenant between God and His people.

The Old Covenant was written in stone, but the New Covenant is written on our hearts. That's what the phrase *"not under the law"* that Paul uses means—the law becomes internal, transforming our hearts so we have no desire to break it, rather than functioning as external rules.

Salvation is a gift, and once received, we begin a process of change as we agree to live a certain way and walk in covenant with God. We should strive to follow God's way of life, refusing to jeopardize our inheritance for the momentary gratification of fleshy desires (Gal. 5.19–21; Heb. 12:14–17). While the new covenant requires faith in Christ, this faith itself is a gift from God, given to all who trust in Christ as their Savior. As a Christian, you can rejoice that you have peace with God, eternal life, are indwelt by the Holy Spirit, and are being conformed to the image of Jesus.

More about God's Covenants:

The Covenant of Works: God made a conditional covenant with Adam in the Garden of Eden. Adam was supposed to obey all God's commands and not eat from the Tree of Knowledge, but Adam rebelled against God and earned instead death and condemnation for himself and all his descendants (Genesis 2:17-18; Genesis 3). Because all humans come from Adam and are represented by him, they are all guilty of failing to keep this covenant. Because God is holy, we are at enmity with God based on our imperfect works—more guilt upon us.

The Covenant of Grace: God promises that a savior will come who will crush the head of the serpent (Satan), (Genesis 3:15). In the Covenant of Grace, people are saved by God's grace through faith in Christ alone because of Christ's complete sacrifice once and for all for sin (Romans 5:12-21, Hebrew 7:27). Through faith in Christ alone, you are declared righteous in God's sight, are forgiven of your sins, have peace with your Creator, and have been gifted all the rights and privileges as God's child for eternity.

"For by grace are ye saved through faith; and that not of yourselves: it is the gift of God. Not of works, lest any man should boast" (Ephesians 2:8-9).

"Therefore being justified by faith, we have peace with God through our Lord Jesus Christ" (Romans 5:1).

The Covenant of Redemption: Without the Covenant of Redemption, the only other covenant in this list that could exist is the Covenant of Works. The Covenant of Redemption was established before the creation of man by the Trinity. The Father sends the Son to do the work of redemption, the Son submits to the Father's will, and the Holy Spirit applies the benefits of the Son's accomplished work to believers. As a reward for his obedience, the Father gifts the Son with glory and an everlasting kingdom (Psalms 110; Isaiah 53; Zechariah 6:12–13; John 17:15). If the Trinity didn't make this pact and keep it, we would all be under God's condemnation without any hope of meeting His holy standards.

Keep in mind that God did not have to save any of us. The covenants gave promise of the Messiah and pointed directly to Jesus Christ (Galatians 3:15–18).

Jesus said, "all things must be fulfilled which were written in the Law of Moses and the Prophets and the Psalms concerning Me." This reveals that all the covenants eventually point to Him (Luke 24:44). Jesus also fulfills God's promises that David's descendants would be rulers forever. Jesus's role in these covenants is key to understanding what covenants mean and how they change between the Old Covenant and the New Covenant.

Moses was commanded to perform wonders before the doubting Israelites so that they would believe that their Lord had called Moses to be the "Old Testament redeemer" (Exodus 4:1–7). After Yahweh had humbled and broken powerful Egypt, he instituted a second covenantal sacrament, the **Passover,** a feast to commemorate Israel's deliverance and at which fathers were to instruct their children about Yahweh's faithful words and deeds (Exodus 12:24–28).

Paul the Apostle, writer of Hebrews, goes so far as to say that God appointed Jesus *"heir of all things"* (Hebrews 1:2). That position as heir to all the covenants put Him in a unique position for sharing those covenants with us. Once the resurrection occurs, we will all inherit the promises as members of God's family (Hebrews 11:8–13, 39–40).

In the New Testament, Paul writes to Gentile believers:

"Remember that at that time you were separate from Christ, excluded from citizenship in Israel and foreigners to the covenants of the promise, without hope and without God in

the world. But now in Christ Jesus you who once were far away have been brought near by the blood of Christ."

In another letter, Paul extends this analogy to say, *"If you belong to Christ, then you are Abraham's descendants, heirs according to the promise"* (Galatians 3:28-29). Jesus makes us part of the family and shares the inheritance with us (Ephesians 2:12-13).

The Ark of the Covenant: God made a <u>conditional</u> covenant with the children of Israel through His servant Moses. He promised good to them and their children for generations if they obeyed Him and His laws, but He always warned of despair, punishment, and dispersion if they were to disobey. To initiate this covenant, He had the people make a chest using acacia wood according to His design. Inside it were the Ten Commandments (the Law) written on two stone tablets, a pot of manna (symbolizing God's constant provision for His people), and the rod of Aaron (Exodus 25:10-22; 16:34; Numbers 17:10; Hebrews 9:4).

The Ark was overlaid inside and out with pure gold and had a Mercy Seat. The term "mercy seat" comes from a Hebrew word meaning "to cover, cleanse, or make atonement for." The mercy seat symbolizes God's throne, where He judges men's conduct, and its name reflects the fundamental nature of His judgments, which always rest on mercy.

Once a year, the high priest entered the Holy of Holies where the Ark was kept and atoned for his sins and the sins of the Israelites (Leviticus 16). The priest sprinkled the blood of a sacrificed animal onto the Mercy Seat to appease the wrath and anger of God for past sins committed. This was the only place in the world where this atonement could occur.

The Ark of the Covenant had a cherub of gold on both ends, and their wings were spread and facing one another. This symbolized the angels' attention and readiness to do God's will. The Ark served as a religious symbol where God could meet with the people and was placed inside the Tabernacle, behind a curtain or veil (Exodus 26:32). The veil served as a separation between the "Holy Place and the Most Holy Place." When Jesus died on the cross, *"The temple curtain was torn in two from top to bottom."* All believers in Jesus Christ could now have confidence that they could draw near to God.

So, where is the Ark of the Covenant now? There are many theories; however, John wrote:

> *"Then God's temple in heaven was opened, and within his temple was seen the Ark of his Covenant. And there came flashes of lightning, rumblings, peals of thunder, an earthquake, and a severe hailstorm"* (Revelation 11:19).

Summary: In the simplest of terms, we have a covenant whenever we have a legally binding agreement. Still, as we can see in the Bible scriptures, covenants also deal with relationships. Adam's relationship with God was based on Adam's obedience, and his failure gave birth to sin and death for us all. Most of the above-mentioned covenants had a condition whereby very good things could happen if agreements were met. However, disaster could result if parties violated the agreement. A blessing could quickly turn into a curse.

Covenants are one of the most critical themes in the Bible—they are the key to God's redemptive plan to restore humanity to its divine calling. Starting in Genesis, God enters into one formal partnership (i.e., covenant) after another with various humans to rescue His world. Covenants are the framework God uses for His relationship with human beings, so if we want to be in a relationship with God, then we'd better make sure we understand the terms of that relationship.

God loves everyone, but He isn't in a loving, friendship relationship with everyone—only with those who keep His covenants.

The Scroll with Seven Seals in Revelation

 John wrote, *"And I saw in the right hand of him that sat on the throne a scroll written within and on the back, sealed with seven seals"* (Revelation 5:1-4).

Early scrolls were made of papyrus, sheep, or goat skin sewn together, often 10-15 feet long. They were usually written on both sides. There are many questions regarding the content of the scrolls; however, they reveal future judgments of God to be poured out on the earth, Christ's Second Coming to rightfully inherit this planet, and His righteous rule in the Millennial Kingdom.

John saw "a strong angel (possibly Gabriel or Michael?) with a loud voice" proclaiming in heaven. The angel's loud voice denotes authority and importance as he announces:

"Who is worthy to open the scroll, and to loose its seals?" After a universal search, *"no man in heaven, nor in earth, neither under the earth the underworld, was able to open the scroll, neither to look on it. John wept much because no man was found worthy to open and to read the scroll, neither to look on it.* But an elder commanded him to stop weeping because one had been found *"to open the scroll, and to loose its seven seals."*

The one qualified to open the seven-sealed scroll is known as "the Lion of the Tribe of Judah," "the Root of David," and as "a Lamb." This holy and qualified one is Jesus Christ.

The Lamb standing in *"the midst of the throne"* (v. 6) stepped down from His throne at the Father's right hand and moved in front of God the Father to receive the scroll. Christ has earned the right to open the scroll based on His Messianic position, holiness, and redemptive death on the cross. He alone has the credentials and is qualified to implement God's wrath and redemptive program recorded in the sealed scroll.

At this point, *"the four living creatures and four and twenty elders fell down before the Lamb"* in worship. *"Blessing, and honor, and glory, and power ... unto Him that sitteth upon the throne, and unto the Lamb forever and ever."*

Jesus takes the scroll and breaks the seals, showing a sequence of events for the next seven years:

1st seal (White horse): This introduces the **Antichrist**. He rides a white horse and speaks of peace at the beginning of the Tribulation. He will have great authority and hold a bow (Revelation 6:1-2).

2nd seal (Red horse): Murder and bloodshed, warfare. Great warfare breaks out on the Earth and is symbolized by the rider with a large sword (Revelation 6:3-4).

3rd seal (Black horse): Famine and starvation. The rider is holding a pair of scales in his hand, and John hears a declaration that people will have to work all day to earn just a little food (Revelation 6:5-6).

4th seal (Pale horse): Death, Hell, and Plague. Its rider is named Death, and Hades was following close behind him. One-fourth of the earth's population is killed by sword, famine, and plague, and by the wild beasts of the Earth (Revelation 6:7-8).

5th seal (Martyrs): Under the altar, the souls of those who were slain for the word of God and the testimony they held. The martyrs cry for the wrath of God. God hears their cries for justice, giving each of them a white robe. The martyrs are told to wait *"until the full number of their fellow servants, their brothers and sisters, were killed just as they had been."* God promises to avenge them, but the time was not yet (Romans 12:19).

6th seal (Great earthquake): The sun became black, and the moon became as blood. The stars fell onto the earth, and every mountain and island were moved out of their places (Revelation 6:12). Survivors of the sixth seal try to take refuge in caves and cry out to the mountains and the rocks, *"Fall on us and hide us from the face of him who sits on the throne and from the wrath of the Lamb! For the great day of their wrath has come, and who can stand?"* (Revelation 16; 17).

After the opening of the sixth of the seven seals, John describes the 144,000 Jewish Witnesses' who will be protected during the Tribulation: Then, in heaven, he sees *"a great multitude that no one could count, from every nation, tribe, people and language, standing before the throne and before the Lamb"* (Revelation 7:1-8). These people wear white robes, hold palm branches, and shout: *"Salvation belongs to our God, who sits on the throne, and to the Lamb."* These people came out of the Great Tribulation; they washed their robes and made them white in the blood of the Lamb.

7th seal (Earthquake and the 7 trumpet and 7 bowl judgments): The judgments leading up to the Tribulation's close are so severe that a solemn silence falls upon all of heaven for about half an hour. The seventh seal introduces the next series of judgments, and John immediately sees seven angels who are handed seven trumpets ready to sound. An eighth angel takes a censer and burns "much incense" in it, representing the prayers of God's people. The angel took the same censer, *"filled it with fire from the altar, and hurled it on the earth; and there came peals of thunder, rumblings, flashes of lightning and an earthquake."*

1st trumpet: Hail and fire mingled with blood are thrown to the earth. One-third of the trees burn up.

2nd trumpet: A great mountain burning with fire is cast into the sea, and 1/3 of the sea becomes blood, 1/3 of the creatures in the sea die, and 1/3 of the ships are destroyed.

3rd trumpet: 1/3 of freshwater rivers and springs become blood-poisoned by a great falling star – "Wormwood."

4th trumpet: 1/3 of the sun, moon, and stars are darkened.

5th trumpet: A star falls from the heavens to the earth and has a key to open the Abyss, and demons are released to run unchecked on the world. The king over them is Abaddon (Hebrew) and Apollyon (Greek). Horse-shaped scorpion-like creatures will sting those not having the seal of God on their foreheads for five months. People will seek death, but it will not come. *Note–This passage parallels Rev. 12-13, namely that Satan falls to earth in Rev. 12 and then gives his authority to the beast rising from the sea in Rev. 13.

6th trumpet: Four fallen angels that were bound at the Euphrates River are released to kill 1/3 of mankind.

7th trumpet: The 7th trumpet includes the 7 bowls' final judgments and all the events leading up to the establishment of the Millennial Kingdom and Jesus as King.

The 7 bowls of God's wrath are poured out on the wicked and the followers of the Antichrist:

1st bowl: Festering sores break out on those having the mark of the Beast.

2nd bowl: The sea becomes as blood and every living creature dies.

3rd bowl: The rivers and streams become blood.

4th bowl: The sun is allowed to scorch people with fire.

5th bowl: The kingdom is plunged into darkness. People gnawed their tongues in agony and cursed God, but refused to repent.

6th bowl: The water from the great Euphrates River is dried up to prepare the way for the kings of the East and their massive armies. Demonic spirits go out to the kings of the earth to gather them for the upcoming battle.

7th bowl: A loud voice from the throne came out of the temple, saying, "It is done!" A massive earthquake split the great city of Babylon into three parts. Huge hailstones fell on people.

A mighty angel came from heaven with a little book in his hand (title deed to the earth), placed his right foot on the land and left foot on the sea, and cried out like a lion's roar:

"Satan may have ruled this kingdom, but Jesus Christ rules it now with sovereign authority."

When he cried out, seven thunders uttered their voices. And from the throne proceeded lightning, thunder, and voices. Seven lamps of fire are burning before the throne, which are the seven spirits of God. Given that thunder is the voice of God in judgment, these sealed instructions may be judgments.

John was forbidden to reveal the content of the seven thunders and told to take the little book and eat it (tasting and eating — meaning hearing and believing). This commandment was to digest the truth of prophecy and be ready to go to the nations with a warning.

Christianity and Judaism

These two religions have similar origins but varying beliefs, practices, and teachings. Both religions have the central idea of **monotheism**, the doctrine or belief that there is only one God, the world's creator. Probably the most significant difference is that **Christianity** believes Jesus (the son of God) is the Messiah who died for our sins, then rose from the dead, and will return from heaven to establish an eternal kingdom with believers. In **Judaism**, Jesus was considered an honorable Jewish rabbi or teacher, but he is not viewed as a divine being or the Messiah.

If born Jewish, you are certainly part of a covenanted community and peoplehood. Although many think of Jews as a race, anyone who accepts the Jewish faith and goes through a conversion process can become part of the Jewish peoplehood. An evangelistic movement is not the Jewish goal, so you see no missionary outreaches toward non-Jews. Christianity is not a race or religion you are born into, but is based on your faith in accepting Jesus Christ as your Lord and Savior.

Christianity believes that all the Bible is "God given," but places special emphasis on Jesus and the New Covenant as recorded in the New Testament. *Judaism emphasizes correct conduct and the Mosaic Law as recorded in the Torah and Tanakh.* Most Christians consider the **Mosaic Law** to have been a necessary intermediate stage. Still, once Jesus's crucifixion occurred, adherence to civil and ceremonial law was superseded by the **New Covenant**. The split between Judaism and Christianity did not come about simply or quickly. Jesus debated issues of Jewish law with the Pharisees, scribes, and chief priests and indeed threatened the authority of these sects with His teachings.

Then, there were the early Jews who seemingly observed the laws of Judaism but accepted that Jesus was indeed the Messiah. There were even laws enacted to further separate these Jewish Christians from the community by prohibiting commerce and specific interaction with them.

The teachings of Jesus attracted even the Gentiles (non-Jews), and the rabbis and upper echelon of the Jewish community regarded this separate religious group as "Nazarenes." Initially, the Romans considered the Christians part of the Jewish people; however, as Christianity spread and gained widespread acceptance, it became the official religion of the Roman Empire.

The following is a quick review of each religion:

Christianity: Originated about 2000 years ago in Judea (present-day Israel). According to 2022 statistics, Christianity is the largest religion in the world, with over 2.5 billion followers (31% of the world population).

Christianity is about the life of Jesus, the Son of God, who came to live in this world as a human. And why would He do this? Because we are all sinners by nature, and we have a broken relationship with our Creator. As sinners, we seek worldly things to fulfill our lives; however, we must develop a closer relationship with God. Jesus came to help us create that relationship.

Jerusalem and Judea are at the heart of what we consider modern-day Israel. During this early period, Judea was a cross-cultural mecca of bustling cities and farms, and the Roman Empire ruled the country. The early group of Jesus followers were called Christians, which comes from "Christianos," meaning "follower of Christ," and from the Greek word "Christos," which means "anointed one," referring to Jesus, whom God anointed.

Acts 11:26 states, *"And in Antioch the disciples were first called Christians."* Other names for Christians are brethren, saints, believers, disciples, or "people of the way." All these terms refer to people who have committed to following Jesus Christ.

In the New Testament, Jesus spoke mainly to a Jewish audience who followed Mosaic Law and Temple traditions. Later, as more heard His message, both Jews and Gentiles became followers, and Christianity was born. His teachings put less emphasis on Jewish law and more on faith and love. Even though many Jews considered Jesus just a teacher, most of Jesus' followers witnessed His miracles and considered Him the promised Messiah.

Christianity is more than a system of religious beliefs; it is a way of life and a dedicated faith handed down from generation to generation. It's about the teachings of Jesus and his dying on a cross for all the world's sins. It's about His resurrection and eternity in a New Heaven and New Earth for those who accept Jesus as their personal savior. It's about having faith in God's words—the Holy Bible.

Judaism: is recognized as one of the world's oldest religions, and it originated about 4000 years ago in the Southern Levant (*modern-day Israel, Palestine, and Jordan*). According to a Pew Research data projection for 2020, Judaism was estimated to have approximately 15.2 million followers worldwide. Hebrews was the original name for the people we now call Jews. The word "Jew" (in Hebrew, "*Yehudi*") is derived from the name Judah, which was the name of one of Jacob's twelve sons. Although not totally accurate, the word "Jew" is commonly used to refer to all the physical and spiritual descendants of Jacob/Israel, as well as to the patriarchs Abraham and Isaac and their wives. "Judaism" refers to their religious beliefs, including defining foods as acceptable (kosher and non-kosher) and setting the calendar of Jewish feasts and fasting days.

In Judaism, the Jewish people are considered "the chosen ones" selected by God. Many claim that this religion was founded by Moses, although Jewish history traces it back to Abraham, a Hebrew man considered to be the father of the Jewish faith.

At that time, people in the Middle East worshipped many gods, and Abraham promoted the central idea that there is only one God. God told Abraham and his wife Sarah that their children would be as plentiful as the stars in the sky and that they would live in the Promised Land. Abraham had a son, Jacob, who was called Israel. Over time, Abraham's descendants came to be known as the Israelites. Much biblical teaching shows that God would care for the Israelites if they obeyed His laws. The enslaved Hebrews who lived in Egypt were led to the Sinai Desert toward the Promised Land by the Hebrew Moses, a specifically chosen one by God. At Mt. Sinai, God gave Moses the Law to guide His people. This law, called the Ten Commandments, would form the basis of the **Torah**, the book of Jewish law. The Torah is part of a larger text known as the **Tanakh** or **Hebrew Bible**.

Judaism is a complex phenomenon and a total way of life for the Jewish people. It includes theology, law, and innumerable cultural traditions. The Jewish people strongly believe they must follow these laws, which govern their daily life. There are also legal books written by rabbis to help determine how the law should apply to a person's life.

Modern Judaism is divided into three main movements:

Orthodox Jews believe that all practices and rituals in the Torah must be obeyed.

Reform Jews believe that followers retain their Jewish identity but take on a more liberal and relaxed approach to many beliefs and practices.

Conservative Judaism takes a somewhat moderate approach and believes that the ancient laws and practices must be interpreted for modern life.

History has not been kind to the Jewish population, and they have experienced much persecution. Some of the worst occurred during World War II when the German Nazis murdered more than six million Jews or a third of the world's Jewish population in what is referred to as the *Holocaust*. Many Jews have returned to their homeland, and in 1948,

Palestine was divided, and a Jewish state of Israel was formed in the land that was once called Canaan. If you look at a map of this region, Israel is surrounded predominantly by unfriendly Muslim countries that hate the Jews and claim rights to some of the lands where the Jewish people live.

Here are a few other similarities and differences between these two religions:

Christians view the Old Testament as the first part of a story completed in the New Testament through the Salvation of Jesus Christ. *In **Judaism**, the central message of the Old Testament focuses on how God called Abraham to lead and set an example of obedience to God's word.*

Christians believe that the New Testament focuses on the life, death, and resurrection of Jesus Christ and is integral to Christianity, *while this is not part of **Judaism** at all.*

Christians and Jews both accept that the Torah represents the first part of the Jewish or Hebrew Bible and comprises the first five books of the Old Testament. In **Christianity**, these five books are considered part of the Old Testament and are no more or less significant than the rest. ***Jews*** *believe that the Torah specifies God's instructions for how Jews should live and that God dictated it to Moses directly.*

Christianity believes that the Holy Trinity consists of God the Father, the Son (Jesus), and the Holy Spirit, and that Jesus became human. ***Judaism*** *is based on the concept of God's Oneness as a sole divine being.*

Christians view Jerusalem as important because this is where Jesus lived, ministered, and was crucified and resurrected. ***Judaism*** *also views Jerusalem as a sacred place of great religious significance since the Temple Mount and other holy sites have stood there.*

Christianity symbols are the Cross, Mary, Ichthys (fish symbol), and Baby Jesus. For **Judaism,** these are the Star of David, Menorah (a seven-branched candelabrum that is described in the Hebrew Bible as having been used in the

Tabernacle and in the Temple in Jerusalem), and the Mezuzah (a small case which contains the handwritten scroll with *Shema* inscribed on it). *Shema* is a Hebrew recitation from the Pentateuch, beginning with "Hear, O Israel, the Lord is our God, the Lord is one." It forms an important part of Jewish evening and morning prayer and is used as a Jewish confession of faith.

In **Christianity**, specific Icons (statues) are used in Orthodox and Catholic denominations, while ***Judaism*** *expressly forbids any form of worship involving statues. Jews are not forbidden to create images, and angels are present in Jewish art. This view derives from a fear that statues are a gateway into idolatry, a severe sin in Judaism.*

Both religions acknowledge history showing that Jesus, his disciples, and members of the oldest Christian churches were Jews. They each followed Jewish traditions and customs, and Jesus often quoted from the Old Testament. Both religions define sin as a rebellion and that there are consequences for one's sins. Both religions believe that God, the ultimate supreme power, is merciful and has made atonement available to erase sin.

Christians worship in a home, church, cathedral, chapel, or basilica while ***Jews*** *worship in synagogues or the Temple of Jerusalem.*

Christians usually worship as a group primarily on Sunday. ***Judaism*** *considers Friday at sunset through Saturday sunset as the Sabbath.*

Christians observe official holidays such as Christmas, New Year, and Easter. ***Jews*** *observe Hanukkah, Passover, Rosh Hashanah, Yom Kippur, Sukkot, Purim, Tisha B'Av, the Three Weeks, and Yom HaShoah (Holocaust Remembrance Day).*

Christians preach that Love is the virtue, while ***Judaism*** *stresses Justice*.

The goal of **Christianity** is to love God and do as commanded. Salvation is based on having faith in Jesus Christ.

For ***Judaism***, *it is an allegiance to a single God, and they believe they are God's chosen people.*

In **Christianity**, Mary is the mother of the son of God, Jesus. *In **Judaism**, since Jews don't consider Jesus as their Messiah, his Jewish mother, Mary, plays no real part in their religion.*

Christianity believes in the virgin birth of Jesus. ***Judaism*** does not mention this in Jewish texts.

In **Christianity**, Jesus's Resurrection is affirmed, while *in **Judaism** it is denied.*

Christianity believes in the Second Coming of Christ. ***Judaism*** *believes in the Coming of a future Messiah.*

Christianity states that Jesus said, "*Whatever goes into a person from outside cannot defile him, since it enters not his heart but his stomach, and is expelled*" Thus, he declared all foods clean (Mark 7:19). ***Judaism*** *states that Jews are required to eat Kosher food (kosher is a term used to describe food that is proper or fit for consumption according to Kashrut, the Jewish dietary law). Meat & dairy cannot be consumed together, and pork is forbidden. There are strict requirements for prayer and ritual butchery of meat. Kosher laws are derived from the Torah.*

Christianity is a faith-based religion. ***Judaism*** *is both a faith practice and an ethnicity, so people are born and retain their Jewish identity, whether they practice it or not.*

Conservative Christians dress modestly. Women wear long skirts or dresses, and men wear dress clothes. *In **Judaism**, Orthodox men almost always wear hats, and Orthodox women dress modestly.*

Christianity does not accept that the Mosaic Law has any authority over Christians. ***Judaism*** *does not accept that the New Testament has any religious authority over Jews.*

The Bible is a collection of 66 books written over a period of more than 1,500 years on three continents by more than 40 authors. These biblical authors lived in different eras and came from many different cultures. Some were highly educated, others had little formal training, and most were just ordinary people. The word Bible is a transliteration of the Greek word "*bíblos*," meaning "book."

It is generally accepted that the original Biblical texts were written in three languages: Hebrew, Aramaic, and *Koine* Greek. The Old Testament was written primarily in Hebrew, with some Aramaic, and the New Testament was written in Greek.

The central message of the Bible is God's story of salvation, which centers on humanity's problem (sin) and God's solution, sending His Son to rescue humanity from this problem.

The Bible is divided into two major divisions: the **Old Testament** (39 books) and the **New Testament** (27 books). Each of these books are further divided into chapters and verses. The 39 books of the Old Testament form the Hebrew Bible of Judaism, while the Christian Bible includes those books and the 27 books of the New Testament.

The books included in the Bible are known as the **Canon,** books regarded as inspired by God and authoritative for faith and life. Canonizing the Old Testament was completed during the days of Nehemiah, Haggai, Zechariah, and Malachi. A council of 120 men, headed by Ezra, formed the many religious writings this group believed to be God's divinely inspired Word. To be included, the text had to be considered divinely inspired, genuine, and written by a prophet or spokesman for God. As the New Testament books were completed, they were judged similarly before being included.

The Bible is God's way of communicating to us the greatest of all love stories. He gave us holy words through human writers, which were then communicated to a vast audience via devoted evangelists. People recognize, and even today, are inspired by these holy words. There have been many attempts to discredit and destroy these sacred words, but the Bible has survived. *"Forever, O Lord, thy word is settled in heaven"* (Psalms 119:89). It's reported that 100 million Bible copies are sold annually. The Bible's complexity can boggle great minds, yet children can understand its simplicity. It's the most widely read, fiercely debated, and probably the most often quoted book in history. No other book shares the uniqueness of the Bible.

The Old Testament talks about the creation of our world, God, and His people before the birth of Christ, and outlines the story of the Jewish nation. (*See list of books and definition below*).

The New Testament tells of the "*good news*" events of Jesus Christ, His life, death, resurrection, ascension, and the continuation of His work in the world by His chosen apostles. The first four books of the New Testament are called "the Gospels." These four books (Matthew, Mark, Luke, and John) give eyewitness accounts of the life of Christ. (**See list of books and definition below*).

The Tanakh or *Mikra* ("what is read") is a collection of 24 books of Hebrew scriptures, primarily written in Hebrew. Tanakh is an acronym derived from the Hebrew letters of the three main sections: Torah, Nevi'im (or Navi), and Ketuvim. Jews revere all the books of the Tanakh as holy and divine works. However, the Torah (Five Books of Moses) holds precedence. Job is considered the earliest book written in the Tanakh. The Tanakh contains the same books as the Old Testament section of the Bible that most Protestant Christians use. However, the order is different, and some books are combined into one volume, so the Tanakh has 24 books instead of the 39 books in the Old Testament. (***See list of books and order below*).

The Torah means teaching. This is what Christians think of as the first five books of the Old Testament—also known as the Pentateuch, the Law, or the Five Books of Moses. The Torah consists of the books of Genesis, Exodus, Leviticus, Numbers, and Deuteronomy. These five books contain the Ten Commandments and the stories of Abraham, Noah, and Moses, among others. When all five books are together, handwritten by a trained scribe, in one parchment scroll, it is called **Sefer Torah** *and is considered very sacred. This precious scroll is read during Jewish prayers in a synagogue. When not used, it is stored in a cabinet or curtained-off* section of the synagogue, called the *Torah ark*. Another form of Torah, printed in book form with commentaries from rabbis (Jewish teachers), is called **Chumash**.

Before Jesus left this world, He stated, "***I will come again***" (John 14:3). This promise is so important that the second coming of Jesus is mentioned 329 times in the Bible. The **word gospel means** "***good news***" and comes from the Greek word "*euaggelion.*"

***The Old Testament (*Jewish Tanakh*)** is comprised of the first 39 books in most Christian Bibles. It contains information regarding the universe's creation, the patriarchs' history, the exodus from Egypt, the formation of Israel as a nation, the subsequent decline and fall of the nation, the Prophets (who spoke for God), and the Wisdom Books. The following is a list of the books and the assumed author:

Genesis: Speaks of beginnings and is foundational to understanding the rest of the Bible. (Moses)

Exodus: Describes the history of the Israelites while leaving Egypt and God's law. (Moses)

Leviticus: The Book of Rules, the Israelites believed they had to follow to be close to their God. (Moses)

Numbers: Tells the story of Israel's journey from Mount Sinai to the plains of Moab. (Moses)

Deuteronomy: Serves as a reminder to God's people about His covenant. (Moses)

Joshua: The story of Israel from the conquest of Canaan to the Babylonian exile. (Joshua)

Judges: Talks about the life of Israel in the Promised Land. (Samuel)

Ruth: Presents an account of the remnants of true faith and piety from the period of the judges. (Samuel)

1 Samuel: Rise and fall of King Saul, and the maturity of young David. (Samuel, Nathan, Gad)

2 Samuel: The rule of King David. (Samuel, Nathan, Gad)

1 Kings: History of God's people under Israel's kings. (Possibly written by the Prophet Jeremiah)

2 Kings: The historical account of Judah and Israel. (Possibly written by the Prophet Jeremiah)

1 Chronicles: Book of history and genealogies. (Possibly written by the prophet Ezra)

2 Chronicles: Account of Israel's history and restoration. (Possibly written by the prophet Ezra)

Ezra: How God's covenant people were restored from the Babylonian exile to the covenant land. (Ezra)

Nehemiah: Closely related to the book of Ezra: chronicles the challenges that the Israelites face. (Nehemiah)

Esther: A Jewish girl who becomes queen.

Job: An account of a righteous man who suffers under terrible circumstances. Some say that Moses is the author, while others suggest Elihu, Solomon, and Ezra wrote it.

Psalms: A collection of songs and poems that represent praises and prayers to God. (King David)

Proverbs: Reference for instructing the young and guiding them in a rewarding way of life. (King Solomon)

Ecclesiastes: Wisdom to examine the human experience and assess the human situation. (King Solomon)

Song of Solomon: Love-inspired words are displayed as one of God's choicest gifts. (King Solomon)

Isaiah: Unveils the full dimensions of God's judgment and salvation. (Isaiah)

Jeremiah: Account of the personal life, ministry, and struggles of the prophet Jeremiah. (Jeremiah)

Lamentations: A series of poetic and powerful laments over the destruction of Jerusalem. (Jeremiah)

Ezekiel: Teaches God's sovereignty over all creation and history. (Ezekiel)

Daniel: Major events in the life of the prophet Daniel and God's sovereign control of history. (Daniel)

Hosea: The prophet's life is a parable of God's faithfulness to an unfaithful Israel. (Hosea)

Joel: Warning to people of Judah about God's coming judgment and blessings through repentance. (Joel)

Amos: The book aimed to announce God's holy judgment on the Kingdom of Israel. (Amos)

Obadiah: Warns the proud people of Edom about the impending judgment coming upon them. (Obadiah)

Jonah: Tells of Jonah's mission to Nineveh, resistance, and imprisonment in a great fish. (Jonah)

Micah: Prediction of the fall of Samaria, and also told of the desolation of Judah. (Micah)

Nahum: The Lord's judgment on Nineveh for her oppression, cruelty, idolatry, and wickedness. (Nahum)

Habakkuk: Dialogue between the prophet and God concerning injustice and suffering. (Habakkuk)

Zephaniah: Announces to Judah God's approaching judgment. (Zephaniah)

Haggai: Encouraged returning exiles to rebuild the temple. (Haggai)

Zechariah: Rebuke the people of Judah and to encourage them to rebuild the temple. (Zechariah)

Malachi: The Great King will come not only to judge people but also to bless them. (Malachi)

**The New Testament is a collection of 27 books, usually placed after the Old Testament in most Christian Bibles. It chronicles Jesus's life and ministry:

Matthew: Writes the "good news" to prove to his Jewish readers that Jesus is their Messiah. (Matthew)

Mark: Tells of the church's persecutions and other sufferings of our Lord. (Mark)

Luke: Written to strengthen the faith of all believers and to answer the attacks of unbelievers. (Luke)

John: Stresses the belief in Jesus Christ, the Son of God, and eternal life. (John)

Acts: The first written history of the Christian church immediately after Jesus's ascension. (Luke)

Romans: The primary theme is presenting the gospel and God's plan of salvation and righteousness. (Paul)

1 Corinthians: Revolves around the theme of problems in Christian conduct in the church. (Paul)

2 Corinthians: Paul explains the true nature and high calling of Christian ministry. (Paul)

Galatians: People are justified by faith in Jesus Christ—by nothing more and nothing less. (Paul)

Ephesians: Tells of God's eternal purpose and grace and God's high goals for the church. (Paul)

Philippians: Gives thanks to Philippians for offering encouragement. (Paul)

The Prison Epistles: Ephesians, Philippians, Colossians, and **Philemon**—are so named because they were written during his incarcerations. (Paul)

1 Thessalonians: Letter to strengthen and encourage the church in Thessalonica. (Paul)

2 Thessalonians: Writes to encourage the church due to persecution. (Paul)

1 Timothy: Instructs Timothy to care for the church at Ephesus. (Paul)

2 Timothy: Concerns about the welfare of churches during this time of persecution under Nero. (Paul)

Titus: Introduced Christianity in Crete when he and Titus visited. Last of the "Pastoral Epistles." (Paul)

Philemon: Paul writes to win Philemon's willing acceptance of the runaway slave Onesimus. (Paul)

Hebrews: The bridge that connects covenants in the Old Testament and the New Testament. (Possibly Paul)

James: Emphasis on vital Christianity characterized by good deeds and a faith that works. (James)

1 Peter: Touches on various doctrines and has much to say about Christian life and duties. (Peter)

2 Peter: Explains that understanding prophecy and salvation is not a matter of opinion. (Peter)

1 John: Letter to expose false teachers and to assure believers of salvation. (John)

2 John: Written to urge discernment in supporting traveling teachers. (John)

3 John: Shows what happens when people follow sound teaching... and when they don't. (John)

Jude: Warning about certain immoral men circulating among them .... false teachers. (Jude)

Revelation: This book contains end-time events and the future reign of Jesus as King. (John)

***The 24 books of the Jewish Tanakh:

<u>Law</u> (*Torah*): These are the books of teaching, the main character of which is Moses. In these books, God chooses Israel to be his special people and lays out his expectations for them **(*Genesis, Exodus, Leviticus, Numbers, and Deuteronomy*).**

Prophets (*Nevi'im*): Here is where we see God's covenant relationship with Israel play out. *The Nevi'im are divided into two groups:*

***The Former Prophets:** Consists of the narrative books of Joshua, Judges, Samuel, and Kings.*

***The Latter Prophets:** Includes the books of Isaiah, Jeremiah, and Ezekiel.*

***The Twelve Minor Prophets:** Hosea, Joel, Amos, Obadiah, Jonah, Micah, Nahum, Habakkuk, Zephaniah, Haggai, Zechariah, and Malachi are considered a single book.*

Writings (*Ketuvim*): This is the third section of the Hebrew Bible. These works of wisdom, poetry, and narrative are arranged to help readers navigate the world in light of God's laws. They helped ancient Jews make decisions, worship God, remember their history, and look forward to a future when the long-awaited Messiah would save them. The books include *Psalms, Proverbs, Job, Song of Solomon, Ruth, Lamentations, Ecclesiastes, Esther, Daniel, Ezra, Nehemiah, and Chronicles.*

Jesus of Nazareth preached the imminent kingdom of the God of Israel, which had been predicted in many of the books of the Jewish prophets. The prophets claimed that God would restore Israel to its past glory in the final days and raise a messiah or "anointed one." This messiah would be a descendant of King David. Some Jews accepted the claim that Jesus was their messiah, but the majority did not.

There are many reasons why most Jews did not join this movement, but probably the most important is that the people wanted a warrior messiah to deliver them from their oppressor, Rome. Jesus served as the "suffering servant" to save the people from their sins. After the death of Jesus, his disciples began teaching his message in Jerusalem and the cities of the Eastern Mediterranean. An essential part of these teachings was that believing in the death, burial, and resurrection of Jesus Christ would result in an eternal afterlife.

Do Human Beings Truly Have Free Will?

If "free will" means that God allows humans to make choices that genuinely affect their destiny, then yes, human beings have free will. The world's current sinful state is directly linked to the choices made by Adam and Eve.

However, free will does not mean that mankind can do anything it pleases. Our choices are limited to what is in keeping with our nature. For example, a man may choose to walk across a bridge or not to walk across it; he may not choose to fly over the bridge—his nature prevents him from flying. Similarly, a man cannot choose to make himself righteous—his sinful nature prevents him from canceling his guilt (Romans 3:23). **The Bible clearly states that we can choose. However, we have the responsibility to choose wisely.**

In the **Old Testament**, God chose a nation (Israel), but individuals within that nation still bore an obligation to choose obedience to God. And individuals outside of Israel could also choose to believe and follow God (e.g., Ruth and Rahab).

In the **New Testament**, sinners are repeatedly told to "repent" and "believe" (Matthew 3:2; 4:17; Acts 3:19; 1 John 3:23). Every call to repent is a call to choose and believe.
Jesus told some unbelievers that they could come to Him if they wanted to. Their problem was that they chose not to.

"You refuse to come to me to have life" (John 5:40).

But how can man, limited by a sinful nature, choose what is good, especially salvation? It is only through the grace and power of God that free will truly becomes "free" in the sense of being able to choose correctly. The **Holy Spirit** works in and through a person's will to regenerate that person. Salvation is God's work, but at the same time, our motives, desires, and actions are voluntary, and we are rightly held responsible for them.

If God knew all the evil things that people would choose to do, why would He give us free will? The answer is that for love to be real, it must not be forced. If we could not reject God, then we would not be able to love Him truly. Perhaps genuine love and good can only exist in a world with an opportunity for genuine rejection and evil.

As mentioned previously, **free will does not mean we are free to do anything we want to do**. When we pray for something, we often hope another's free will will be affected. If an evil country invades a peaceful country, and we pray for their defeat, we are praying that the evil country will not be able to do what it has chosen to do with its free will.

There are spiritual limitations to our "free will." Romans 8:5–8 states:

> *"Those who live according to the flesh have their minds set on what the flesh desires; but those who live in accordance with the Spirit have their minds set on what the Spirit desires. The mind governed by the flesh is death, but the mind governed by the Spirit is life and peace. The mind governed by the flesh is hostile to God; it does not submit to God's law, nor can it do so. Those who are in the realm of the flesh cannot please God."*

From the context, you would think that those who "*live according to the flesh*" can't be saved. Their wills are in bondage to sin, and so sin is all they want to do. They cannot submit to God's law. If this is the case, who then can be saved? **"All things are possible with God"** (Mark 10:27).

The Lord works to energize a person's spirit and give them a desire to repent (Acts 16:14). Sinners do not do this on their own but only under the convicting power of the Holy Spirit. If otherwise, the saved could boast that they possessed some wisdom or moral superiority that caused them to choose to repent and believe when confronted with the facts, even while so many others continue to reject the gospel.

"We are saved by grace, and no one can boast" (Ephesians 2:8–9). God is not obligated to save anyone, yet He desires that all be saved and repent.

He offers salvation to everyone, yet He will not force anyone to come to Him. Coming to faith in Christ makes us desire the things of God, yet Christians still have an old nature that pulls them in the other direction (Titus 2:11).

God created a world where people could choose to disobey, and He allows people today to continue to rebel against Him. The concept of redemption is described as the action of saving or being saved from sin, error, or evil, and giving praise to God's glory (Ephesians 1:14). As should be expected, this doctrine is wholly unsatisfying to those who are in rebellion against God and have no desire to give Him glory.

God does not force people to accept or reject Him. After finishing a long section on God's control and human choice, Paul states this: *"To him be the glory forever! Amen"* (Romans 11:36). And Paul ends the letter to the Romans with, *"To the only wise God be glory forever through Jesus Christ! Amen"* (Romans 16:27).

In the Bible, the concept of free will is a central theme. Individuals are shown exercising their free will to follow God's commandments or rebel against them. This power to choose is not something that should be considered lightly, because what comes along with the power to choose is the reality that there are consequences for your choices.

"You say, 'I am allowed to do anything'—but not everything is good for you. You say, 'I am allowed to do anything'—but not everything is beneficial" (1 Corinthians 10:23).

Predestination vs. Free Will?

Most people don't even want to discuss this topic. One group may have such strong feelings that they virtually reject the thoughts of the other group before discussing them. We just studied the concept of free will and a person's choice of either following God's commandments or rebelling against them. So, what does the Bible say about Predestination vs. Free Will?

Predestination in the Bible refers to the doctrine that God has eternally chosen those whom he intends to save. It implies that God has a purpose determined long before it is brought to pass. Predestination is God's sovereign will determining certain things to happen beforehand.

> *"For God knew his people in advance, and he chose them to become like his Son, so that his Son would be the firstborn among many brothers and sisters. And having chosen them, he called them to come to him. And having called them, he gave them right standing with himself"* (Romans 8:29-30).

When you look at this verse, it says **God foreknew**. This means God knew in advance those who would choose to follow him and those who would choose not to follow him. The ones he knew in advance are the ones he predestined to be conformed to the image of his Son. In other words, ***God's predestining is based on his foreknowledge, not his random selection***. This understanding allows God to remain just and still hold people accountable for their choices.

> *"Having predestinated us unto the adoption of children by Jesus Christ to himself, according to the good pleasure of his will, To the praise of the glory of his grace, wherein he hath made us accepted in the beloved. In whom we have redemption through his blood, the forgiveness of sins, according to the riches of his grace; Wherein he hath abounded toward us in all wisdom and prudence; Having made known unto us the mystery of his will, according to his*

good pleasure which he hath purposed in himself: That in the dispensation of the fulness of times he might gather together in one all things in Christ, both which are in heaven, and which are on earth; even in him: In whom also we have obtained an inheritance, being predestinated according to the purpose of him who worketh all things after the counsel of his own will" (Ephesians 1:5-11).

Remember, in our previous study, free will does not mean we have absolute freedom to do anything. The Bible teaches that **without Christ, we are "*dead in our trespasses and sins*"** (Ephesians 2:1). If we are spiritually dead, surely that can impact our decision-making.

"For the grace of God has appeared that offers salvation to all people" (Titus 2:11). ***"God wants everyone to be saved and to come to the knowledge of the truth"*** (1 Timothy 2:4).

In the Bible, God repeatedly calls on us to exercise our free will and trust in Christ for salvation. We should pursue obedience to those commands regardless of how well we do or don't understand them. Here are a few more predestination passages:

"For he chose us in him before the creation of the world to be holy and blameless in his sight. In love he <u>predestined</u> us for adoption to sonship through Jesus Christ, in accordance with his pleasure and will" (Ephesians 1:4-5).

"And if the Lord had not cut short the days, no human being would be saved. But for the sake of the <u>elect, whom he chose</u>, he shortened the days" (Mark 13:20).

"Therefore, as <u>the elect of God</u>, holy and beloved, put on tender mercies, kindness, humility, meekness, longsuffering" (Colossians 3:12).

"For we know, brothers and sisters loved by God, that <u>hehas chosen you</u>" (1 Thessalonians 1:4).

"Therefore I endure all things for the elect's sakes, that they may also obtain the salvation which is in Christ Jesus with eternal glory" (2 Timothy 2:10).

We all know that many things in the Bible seem to be mysteries. This predestination issue is certainly one of them.

Regardless of how you view predestination, you have a choice to make, and that choice you make will mean an eternity with our Lord or an eternity in Hell.

We should never get distracted by whether it is free will or predestination. The real issue is to make the gospel available to as many people as possible.

Conclusion: God knows in advance who will choose to follow Him and who will choose not to. He predestined them to be conformed to the image of his Son.

As previously stated, God's predestining is based on His foreknowledge, not random selection. This understanding allows God to remain just while holding people accountable for their choices.

Calendars Throughout the World

The calendar is basically a chart or series of pages showing the days, weeks, and months of a particular year, or informative seasonal information. The actual word "calendar" has a somewhat unusual history. Some data shows the word taken from "calends" or "kalends," the term used for the first day of the month in the Roman calendar. This relates to "calare," referring to the calling or announcement that the new moon was just seen.

In Latin, *"calendarium"* means "account book or register", and accounts were settled, and debts were collected on the calends of each month. The Latin term was adopted in Old French as *"calendier"*; the Middle English 13th century used *"calender"*; and then Early Modern English adopted the spelling *"calendar."*

The **Lunar calendar** months correspond to cycles of Moon phases. This period is sometimes called a lunar year because there are about twelve lunations in a solar year. A common purely lunar calendar is the *Islamic* calendar or *Hijri Qamari* calendar.

The **Lunisolar calendar** combines lunar and solar calendars. Its date indicates both the Moon's phase and the time of the solar year (the position of the Sun in the Earth's sky). Examples include the Babylonian, Hindu, Hebrew, and Chinese calendar families.

The **Solar calendar** measures the time it takes the Earth to revolve around the sun (one orbit is 365.25 days). Dates on this calendar indicate the season and are based on the Earth's position and proximity to the sun. The Gregorian calendar, widely accepted as a standard worldwide, is an example of a solar calendar.

When viewing various calendar dates, **AD or A.D**. stands for ***Anno Domini*** (Latin for "In the year of the Lord") and is a label for numbering years <u>after Christ's Birth</u>.

BC or B.C. means "<u>Before Christ</u>." *Christ was born is AD 1, and the year before is labeled 1 BC.*

CE is an abbreviation for "<u>Common Era</u>," and BCE is short for "Before Common Era." The Common Era begins with the *year 1 in the Gregorian calendar.* CE and BCE are used similarly to the traditional abbreviations AD and BC.

Religious neutrality was the primary rationale behind Jewish academics' adoption of BCE/CE and continues to be its most widely cited justification. The movement towards BCE/CE has not been universally accepted, and BC/AD is still more widely used.

So, how did all this calendar stuff get started? Why are there so many, and what are the differences? Let's look at a few and discuss their history and usage.

Jewish or Hebrew Calendar: The Guinness Book of World Records honors the oldest calendar still in use as the **Hebrew** calendar. This lunisolar calendar, which is based on lunar months, but years are based on solar years. has been used regularly since the 9th century BCE. Along with tracking Jewish religious holidays, the ***Jewish*** calendar basically divides the year according to agricultural activities such as sowing, reaping, pruning, and storage.

The Jewish "leap year," which occurs seven times in a 19-year cycle, is used so the lunar-based Jewish year will remain aligned with the solar seasons. The ancient **Hebrews** did not record dates by citing the month and day of an event, but by referencing the date to some significant event such as the accession year of a reigning king (2 Kings 15:17): *"In the thirty-ninth year of Azariah's reign over Judah, Menahem son of Gadi became king of Israel, and ..."*

Only as Julius Caesar's calendar reforms became embedded in the culture did people change from this long-standing method to a more standardized system.

Roman Calendar: According to legend, **Romulus** (Rome's founder and first king) instituted this calendar. However, it was probably a product of evolution from the **Greek** lunar calendar, which in turn was derived from the **Babylonians**.

The original Roman calendar consisted of 10 months and a year of 304 days that started in March. It was initially called Martius and was named after the Roman god of war. The Roman calendar was very complicated and required people to decide when days should be added or removed to keep the calendar in sync with the astronomical seasons.

Julian Calendar: In 45 BC, *Julius Caesar* introduced this calendar (*sometimes called the "Old Style" calendar*) to replace the Roman calendar. Caesar's calendar was based on the tropical year (how long it takes the Earth to travel around the sun), split the year into 12 months, and introduced the concept of a leap year. This calendar was used in Europe and northern Africa before the world gradually switched to the Gregorian calendar around 1582.

Gregorian Calendar: (*Greg-gor-e-n*) This *"New Style" calendar* is the most used in the modern world and was introduced by Pope Gregory XIII. The Gregorian calendar, like the Julian calendar, is solar (365 days) with 12 months of 28-31 days each. For leap years, a day is added to February. The Pope's main goal with his new calendar was to realign the date for Easter with the proper season. The Gregorian calendar was first adopted in Italy, Poland, Portugal, and Spain in 1582, and the United States adopted the calendar in 1752.

Liturgical Calendar: (Le-tur-the-cul) A system used in Catholic churches to mark when feast days, including celebrations of saints, are to be observed, and which portions of Scripture are to be read either in an annual cycle or a cycle of several years. Four major seasons guide the liturgical calendar—***Advent, Christmas, Lent, and Easter***. The period outside these seasons is called "Ordinary Time" or "time during the year." The term Advent is taken from the Latin word *"adventus"*, which means "arrival" or "coming" and was translated from the Greek word *"Parousia"* (*pair-oo-sia*), meaning "a coming" or "a presence."

The words of Paul can be used to govern these observances:

"One person considers one day more sacred than another; another considers every day alike. Each of them should be fully convinced in their own mind. Whoever regards one day as special does so to the Lord. Whoever eats meat does so to the Lord, for they give thanks to God; and whoever abstains does so to the Lord and gives thanks to God. For none of us lives for ourselves alone, and none of us dies for ourselves alone. If we live, we live for the Lord; and if we die, we die for the Lord. So, whether we live or die, we belong to the Lord. For this very reason, Christ died and returned to life so that he might be the Lord of both the dead and the living" (Romans 14:5–9).

Advent Calendar: Let me add this calendar because it has a very unusual history. In Germany in the late 19th century, a mother made an Advent Calendar for her son Gerhard Lang, which was comprised of 24 tiny sweets stuck onto cardboard. Lang never forgot the excitement he felt when he was given his Advent calendar at the beginning of each December, and how it reminded him every day that the most fantastic celebration of the whole year was approaching.

During his adult years, he opened a printing office and produced what is thought to be the first-ever printed Advent Calendar with a small colored picture for each day of the month. Later, he put pictures into little shuttered windows for the children to open daily to heighten their sense of expectation.

The Advent Calendar was extremely popular, but unfortunately, it ended during the First World War when cardboard was strictly rationed and only allowed to be used for purposes necessary to the war effort. It was reintroduced following the end of the Second World War. You might also see the Advent wreath with five candles, with one candle lit each Sunday and the fifth, the Christ Candle, lit on December 24.

More interesting items about calendars:

The Sumerians were thought to be the first to use calendars in Mesopotamia during the Bronze Age. Each month on this calendar has 29 or 30 days, depending on whether the first day has a full moon. Regardless, there were always 12 months in a year. The Egyptian, Assyrian, and Elamite calendars followed the Sumerian calendar.

Many ancient calendar systems were based on the **Babylonian** calendar from the Iron Age, among them the Persian Empire calendar system, which gave rise to the Zoroastrian and Hebrew calendars. The Babylonians created a seven-day week based on the seven celestial bodies they saw in the sky—the Sun, Moon, Mercury, Venus, Mars, Jupiter, and Saturn. It is thought that they also introduced the 60-minute hour.

The ancient **Mayans and other Mesoamericans** developed a calendar that lasted two simultaneous years. The "*Tzolkin*" was 260 days, and the "*Haab*" was 365 days. The months in each year have between 13 and 20 days. Together, they form a longer cycle of 18,980 days, or 52 years of 365 days, called "Calendar Round."

Some may have heard that the ancient Maya predicted the world would end on 21 December 2012. That is not true, because on the next day, the Maya believed that a new cycle would begin again. There was to be no end to the world.

In the 11th century, Omar Khayyam produced a calendar in Persia that measured the length of the year as 365.24219858156 days. Given that the length of the year changes in the sixth decimal place over a person's lifetime, this is outstandingly accurate. For comparison, the length of the year at the end of the 19th century was 365.242196 days, while today (1999) it is 365.242190 days.

The ancient **Egyptian** calendar only had three seasons and was noted by agriculture and the flooding of the Nile River. The first season, A*khet*, was when the Nile flooded; the second season, P*eret*, was when crops began to grow; and the third season, S*hemu*, corresponded with the start of the harvest.

The **Muslim or Islamic** calendar is also known as the *Hijri* calendar and was created in 638 CE (six years after the Prophet Muhammad's death). It is a lunar-based calendar with 12 months, each corresponding with the appearance of a new moon. The day Muhammad migrated from *Makkah* to *Al Madina El Monawara* is Year One. This site is celebrated for containing the mosque of Muhammad and ranks as the second-holiest city of Islam (after Mecca). Ramadan is the ninth and most sacred month for fasting and celebrating *Allah*, the Arabic name for God. At the end of the month, a major holiday feast called *Eid al-Fitr* is celebrated.

Scholars theorize that the monument **Stonehenge** in England was likely used as an ancient solar calendar, able to track days and months. Stonehenge consists of an outer and inner ring of standing stones that archaeologists think were constructed around 3000 BC to 2000 BC. It's a mystery who built it, but the stones were set up to frame the two most important events in the solar cycle: the midwinter sunset (winter solstice) and the midsummer sunrise (summer solstice). The solstice happens when the sun reaches its maximum or minimum declination, marked by the longest and shortest days near June 21 and December 22.

In the Chinese lunisolar calendar, years are named after a repeating cycle of 12 animals. The 12 zodiac animals, in order, are Rat, Ox, Tiger, Rabbit, Dragon, Snake, Horse, Goat, Monkey,

Rooster, Dog, and Pig. Each year is associated with an animal sign according to the 12-year cycle. 2022 was the Year of the Tiger, and 2023 will be the Year of the Rabbit, more precisely, the Year of the Water Rabbit. According to Chinese astrology, the Rabbit symbolizes patience and luck.

So what about New Year's and New Year's Eve Around the World?

According to History.com, the earliest recorded festivities in honor of the New Year date back 4,000 years to ancient Babylon. The first day of the New Year was the first new moon following the vernal equinox—two moments in the year when the Sun is exactly above the Equator and day and night are of equal length. The occasion was marked by a religious festival spanning 11 days, with a different daily ritual. Many calendars have set the first day of the New Year as an agricultural or astronomical event.

Romans celebrated the New Year by offering sacrifices, exchanging gifts, decorating their homes with laurel branches, and giving or attending parties. New Year's Day in Ethiopia begins in September, when the country's long rainy period has ended. In **Germany**, New Year's Eve is called "Silvester" (or Sylvester), after the 4th century Pope Sylvester I, and is celebrated with fireworks, champagne, and social gatherings.

Israel celebrates the Jewish New Year with *Rosh Hashanah*, an important two-day religious holiday typically occurring in September or October of each year. Since 1873, the **Japanese** New Year has been celebrated according to the Gregorian calendar. At midnight on December 31, the Buddhist temples in Japan ring their bells 108 times to symbolically remove the 108 human sins in Buddhist belief. Another custom is making boiled sticky rice cakes, called *mochi,* which are eaten at the beginning of January.

In **Russia**, children wake up on New Year's Day to gifts from Grandfather Frost (*Ded Moroz*), the Russian Santa Claus. The traditional decorated tree is considered a New Year's tree and stays up until the Russian Orthodox Christmas on January 7th. **Scotland** has an old superstition called *"First Footing,"* meaning that good luck comes if the first person to set foot in your house on New Year's Day is a tall, dark-haired man, especially if he brings a gift of food or coal. This will ensure no lack of food or warmth in the household. In **Thailand,** a ceremony called *"Songkran"* is celebrated on New Year's Day and involves washing statues of Buddha and the hands of elders to ensure they enter the New Year spiritually clean.

The **Chinese** New Year, also known as *Spring Festival* or *Lunar New Year*, changes its dates yearly because it follows the lunar calendar. Usually, it falls on a day between mid-January and mid-February. In 2023, the Chinese New Year falls on January 22. The 2023 year of the Water Rabbit begins on January 22nd and ends on February 9th, 2024. The sign of the Rabbit is a symbol of longevity, peace, and prosperity in Chinese culture, and 2023 is predicted to be a year of hope. The rabbit's association with the moon in Chinese mythology has created a sign that is partial to beauty. They are sensitive creatures who place great importance on peace and tranquility. The rabbit is also the sign that indicates longevity and fortune. The rabbits are quietly determined, talented, and wildly ambitious. There are five types of Rabbits: *Water Rabbit (2023), Wood Rabbit, Fire Rabbit, Earth Rabbit, and Gold Rabbit.*

*Malaysia***:** The Lunar New Year is one of the most exciting festivals in Malaysia. This festival of renewal is of huge religious and cultural significance in the Southeast Asian nation, where a quarter of the population claims Chinese ancestry. Tourists who visit Malaysia should visit Penang, especially the Chulia Street area. Yee Sang, a special dish only served during Chinese New Year, contains many different vegetables and other ingredients. Once ready, people will toss the shredded bits into the air using their chopsticks. It must be tossed high into the air, reflecting the good luck, health, and prosperity they will receive.

The **Korean** New Year is *Seollal* or *Lunar New Year's Day*. Seollal is the first day of the lunar calendar and generally occurs in January or February on the second new moon after the winter solstice. Celebration is believed to have started to let in good luck and ward off evil spirits throughout the year. It is one of the most important traditional holidays in North and South Korea, and the celebration usually lasts three days.

The **Vietnamese** New Year is the *Tết Nguyên Đán,* which roughly translates into English as "the first morning of the first day," and has been celebrated for thousands of years. **Babylonians** celebrated the New Year about 4,000 years ago, but not on the first of January. Their New Year began with the first new moon after the first day of spring or the middle of March and lasted for eleven days, each with its unique celebration. **India** traditionally celebrates the New Year on the first of March every year; however, this date was switched to January 1 as it is considered to have more religious significance. This is a multi-cultural country, and every state in India has its own history behind the New Year celebration. Therefore, each state follows its tradition and culture to celebrate the occasion. Celebrations include: *Chaitra, Navreh, Ugadi, Lord Brahma, Cheti Chand, Gudi Padwa, Varuna*, and *Nava Varsha.*

The **Iranian** New Year in the *Baháʼí* calendar occurs on the vernal equinox (day and night of equal length) on March 20 or 21 and is called *Naw-Rúz or Nowruz.* The Iranian tradition was also passed on to Central Asian countries, including Kazakhs, Uzbeks, and Uighurs, and is one of eleven holy days for those of the Baháʼí Faith.

In the **United States**, New York City has the famous Times Square ball that begins to drop one minute before midnight. The history of this renowned ball is fascinating. *"Time balls"* were invented so that sailors could adjust their chronometers, or timepieces. With a telescope, they would scope the harbor and watch for a time ball to drop at a specific time, usually noon or 1 p.m. The ball was installed for the first time in 1829 in Portsmouth, England. The U.S. Naval Observatory followed suit and began dropping a time ball in 1845 in Washington's Foggy Bottom neighborhood. Soon, many port towns and cities adopted the practice.

The New York Times building in midtown Manhattan was completed in 1904, and New Year's Eve celebrations moved to this area. Crowds had previously gathered at Trinity Church in downtown Manhattan to hear the bells ring at midnight. Instead of chimes, The New York Times company produced a midnight fireworks spectacle that proved effective but disastrous when hot ashes from the fireworks rained down onto the streets. The New York Police Department banned future fireworks, so Walter Palmer, The New York Times' chief electrician, was approached to find a new light display. The result was a 700-pound ball made of iron and wood with 100 25-watt light bulbs attached to its surface. At midnight, the ball descended the repurposed mainmast of the battleship USS New Mexico with a system of pulleys.

Over time, the ball was redesigned, with aluminum replacing iron. Computer controls were added to the LED strobe and rotating pyramid mirrors. The ball now weighs about 11,875 pounds and is 12 feet in diameter. Those 100 25-watt light bulbs have been replaced by 2,688 Waterford Crystals that refract the light of 32,256 Philips LEDs. The crystals are carefully crafted with a special meaning for each new year.

We could never talk about this time of the year without mentioning food. New Year's Eve means lots of celebrations worldwide, which usually means lots of eating. And keep in mind, there are a few foods that will supposedly bestow your life with luck and prosperity.

Pomegranates are associated with fertility and life. In Greek culture, a pomegranate is placed outside the home and smashed on New Year's Day. The more seeds that scatter during the initial smash, the luckier the year ahead will be. **Black-eyed peas** are part of the traditional meal in the South, eaten on New Year's Day. Some say the shape of black-eyed peas represents coins and therefore encourages wealth. Others trace the humble black-eyed pea back to the Civil War era, where the beans are said to have prevented families from starvation.

Leafy greens are reminiscent of dollar bills and are believed to bring wealth. **Cornbread** is considered lucky due to its golden-brown color, which is said to bring gold and wealth in the upcoming year. **Noodles** are consumed across Asia and symbolize longevity. In Chinese culture, yi mein noodles, the chewy and brightly yellow egg noodles, are stir-fried and are said to encourage a long life. In Spain and Mexico, it is traditional to eat twelve **Grapes** at the stroke of midnight, representing the twelve months within a calendar year. The luck you'll have will depend on the sweetness of the grapes. **Round cakes** are typically considered lucky due to their shape; they resemble coins and are thought to bring wealth in the new year.

Pork comes from animals that root forward as they sniff out and eat food, symbolizing progress. The fattiness of pork is also related to luxury and wealth, so don't hesitate to fry up some bacon to start the New Year. **Lentils** are eaten worldwide for the new year because the tiny legumes are said to look like little coins, which will bring prosperity in the coming year.

Fish represent abundance since they swim in large schools, and their shimmery scales resemble coins. In some Eastern European cultures, the scales are saved and placed in a wallet to acquire more wealth. **Oranges and tangerines** are typically passed out during the Lunar New Year to bring prosperity.

Regardless of the culture, New Year's Eve and New Year's Day are important holidays worldwide. They represent putting aside the old year and bringing in a new year of good health and happiness.

Dispensations

The word dispensation is commonly taught to be a "**period of time**," or its Greek equivalent of "*oikonomia*." (oi–ko–no–mia —thought of as "divine economy." The term means stewardship, administration, or careful management of goods or resources.

God is the owner of all creation and establishes a set of directions that He expects people to believe and obey in an orderly fashion. This information is given to mankind to define their faith and obedience over an established period of time. Most theologians believe seven dispensations are identified, although the number can vary quite a bit.

God does not change, but dispensations change because man changes. The word "dispensation" appears four times in the King James Bible:

> *"For if I do this thing willingly, I have a reward: but if against my will, a dispensation of the gospel is committed unto me"* (1 Corinthians 9:17).

> *"That in the dispensation of the fulness of times he might gather together in one all things in Christ, both which are in heaven, and which are on earth; even in him . . ."* (Ephesians 1:10).

> *"If ye have heard of the dispensation of the grace of God which is given me to you-ward . . ."* (Ephesians 3:2).

> *"Whereof I am made a minister, according to the dispensation of God which is given to me for you, to fulfil the word of God . . ."* (Colossians 1:25).

Each dispensation reveals a pattern involving the stewards of the dispensation, their responsibility, a specific period, a failure, the resulting judgment, and God's grace. Dispensationalism also makes a clear distinction between

Israel and the Church. So, what responsibilities does God expect us to honor during these various timeframes?

1st dispensation is called the **Dispensation of Innocence** and covers the period of Adam and Eve in the Garden of Eden (Genesis 1:28-30; 2:15-17). The primary responsibility here was to obey God. This is the shortest of the dispensations. God created man to live in perfect harmony with Himself, and nothing was known of imperfection or evil. In this dispensation, God commands us to be fruitful and increase in number, fill the earth and subdue it, rule over the fish in the sea and the birds in the sky, and over every living creature that moves on the ground. Man is to work and care for the Garden of Eden, and can eat from any tree in the garden except the tree of the knowledge of good and evil. God warns of the punishment of physical and spiritual death for disobedience.

God pronounced judgment on Adam and Eve, but He also showed mercy by killing an innocent animal and providing skins to atone for their sin. The slaughter of the animals introduced the biblical principle "*without the shedding of blood there is no forgiveness*" (Hebrews 9:22).

This dispensation ended when Adam and Eve disobeyed God by eating the forbidden fruit and were expelled from the garden. Adam and Eve were the stewards, and the period lasted from man's creation to his temptation and fall.

2nd dispensation is called the **Dispensation of Conscience.** Adam and Eve made a terrible decision in the garden, and everyone born has inherited their sin since then. In this dispensation, you will find the curse on the serpent, a change in womanhood and childbearing, a curse on nature, the imposing of challenging work on mankind to produce food, and the promise of Christ as the seed who will bruise the serpent's head (Satan). During the dispensation of Conscience, mankind only became worse. Man was supposed to choose to do good and approach God by means of a blood sacrifice.

It was in this period that the first death occurred when Cain slew his brother Abel. God had accepted Abel's animal sacrifice, but not Cain's grain sacrifice. Before the murder, God warned Cain of impending sin and told him that he could still choose to do well by bringing a proper sacrifice. Cain refused to follow God's plan, and shortly thereafter, he killed his brother. He lied to God about his crime and was banished by the Lord from the settled country. According to the Book of Jubilees, Cain died at the age of 730 when his stone house fell on him and killed him.

"The Lord saw how great man's wickedness on the earth had become, and that every inclination of the thoughts of his heart was only evil all the time" (Genesis 6:5).

God's solution at this point was to destroy man and all land-dwelling animals from the face of the earth. But Noah found favor (grace) in the eyes of the Lord. For 120 years, as Noah built the Ark, he warned the people of God's coming wrath, but they ignored him. Then, the worldwide flood came, and the wicked were destroyed. God extended grace to Noah and his family (8 people), established His covenant with them (Genesis 6:14-22), and brought them into a new dispensation. <u>Stewards</u> Cain, Seth, and their families. This period lasted from man's expulsion from the Garden of Eden until the Flood, about 1,656 years.

3rd dispensation is the **Dispensation of Human Government**, which began in Genesis 8. God had destroyed life on earth with a flood, saving just one family to restart the human race. At this point, God divinely appointed a human agency known as civil government to restrain evil and protect man from his sinful nature. The survivors of the flood, Noah, his wife, their three sons, and their wives, began to repopulate the earth. The son Shem would become the father of the Mediterranean region dwellers and eventually the Jews. The word Semitic comes from the Latin word for "Shem." The son

Ham and his descendants spread into Africa, and the son Japheth spread into Eurasia (Europe and Asia).

God made Noah and his family responsible for protecting the sanctity of human life. "*Whoever sheds man's blood, by man shall his blood be shed, for in the image of God He made man*" (Genesis 9:6). In doing this, God established the orderly rule of mankind for the good of society. Capital punishment is the most potent function of human government, and man is still responsible for using this authority to enforce righteousness.

Sin (lawlessness) continued in the third dispensation, and it was a time of great idolatry and moral degradation. The Tower of Babel was the height of disobedience against God during this period. God ultimately divided humanity into different language groups and scattered them throughout the earth. God also established a covenant with Noah that He would never again destroy the world by water, and the sign of this promise would be the rainbow. <u>Stewards</u> were Noah and his descendants, and the period was from the Flood to the confusion of tongues at Babel, about 429 years.

4th dispensation, called the **Dispensation of Promise**, began with Abraham, continued through the lives of the patriarchs, and ended with the Exodus of the Jewish people from Egypt. It is called the dispensation of "Promise" because of the covenant made with Abraham, who lived in the "*land of promise*" (Hebrews 6:13; 11:9). A great nation of God's chosen people was developed during this dispensation, and we see the promise of the Abrahamic Covenant. This unconditional covenant stated that Abraham's name would be great and from him would come a great nation that God would bless with natural and spiritual prosperity. God would bless those who blessed Abraham's descendants and curse those who cursed them. The sign of the covenant was circumcision, which was confined to the Hebrew people and the 12 tribes of Israel. As the patriarch, Abraham had issues such as fathering Ishmael and deceiving others in Egypt about his wife Sarah. Over time, the Hebrew people decided not to believe God's promises to Abraham concerning guidance, protection, and blessings. They took it upon themselves to manage their lives without God's help. But the ever-patient God provided grace through Moses, through Passover protection, and He met their material needs.

In Exodus 19:4, God reminds the Israelites of His grace: *"You yourselves have seen what I did to Egypt, and how I carried you on eagles' wings and brought you to myself."* The dispensation of Promise ended at Mt. Sinai, where God gave Abraham's people the Law to govern them in yet another manner. <u>The patriarchs Abraham, Isaac, and Jacob were the stewards, and the period lasted</u> about 430 years.

5th dispensation is called the **Dispensation of Law**. During this dispensation, God dealt specifically with the Jewish nation through the Mosaic Covenant, which is referred to as the Law (Exodus 19-23; John 19:30). This was Gods only conditional covenant with Israel, and the blessings and success depended upon the people's obedience to the Law (Exodus 19:5). It did not take long for the Law to be broken, as proved by the golden calf in Exodus 32. The apostle Paul said the Law was given to Israel, not the Gentiles or the Church (Romans 2:14; Ephesians 2:11-12).

The dispensation involved temple worship directed by priests, with further direction spoken through God's prophets. Eventually, due to the people's disobedience to the covenant, the tribes of Israel lost the Promised Land and were subjected to bondage.

The Law was a temporary covenant to be made null and void by the institution of the New Covenant (Jeremiah 31:32; Hebrews 8:13; 10:9). The Law was added "because of transgressions until the Seed to whom the promise referred had come" (Galatians 3:19). While the Abrahamic Covenant continues and has not yet been completely fulfilled (even to this day), God changed course with His chosen people Israel at Mt. Sinai. God added the Law, with it a new dispensation with a beginning and an ending (Romans 10:4). The dispensation of

Law is over. The people of Israel were never meant to be saved by keeping the Law (Romans 3:20). The Law was established to define sin, help them govern their earthly lives, and lead them to the coming Savior—Jesus Christ. Israel misinterpreted the purpose of the Law and sought righteousness by doing good deeds and having ceremonial ordinances rather than believing in God's grace (Romans 9:31; 10:3; Acts 15:1).

Perhaps it is because they were so focused on attaining their holiness that they rejected their Messiah (John 1:11). Israel has a long history of violating God's Law, however, Jesus stated that the Law was still fulfilled:

"***Do not think that I have come to abolish the Law or the Prophets; I have not come to abolish them but to fulfill them***" (Matthew 5:17).

Jesus gave His life so that we could be saved.

"*A man is not justified by observing the law, but by faith in Jesus Christ. So we, too, have put our faith in Christ Jesus that we may be justified by faith in Christ and not by observing the law, because by observing the law no one will be justified*" (Galatians 2:16).

<u>Moses and the nation of Israel were the stewards, and this period lasted almost 1,500 years—from Mt. Sinai until it was fulfilled by Jesus's death and resurrection</u>. Some scholars believe that this dispensation will continue during the Millennium, with some modifications.

6th dispensation, the one in which we now live, is the **Dispensation of Grace** (John 19:31 to Revelation 3:22). This dispensation is often referred to as the **Church Age** because it is during this era that Jesus is building His Church (Matthew 16:18). It began at **Pentecost** (Acts 2), and will end when all who are born again by the baptism of the Holy Spirit are raptured out of this world to be with Jesus (1 Thessalonians 4:13-18). The Church is mentioned again in Revelation 19 as returning to earth with the Lord Jesus at His Second Coming.

Since the dispensation of Innocence, God has appealed to mankind to do right. The dispensation of Conscience lasted about 1,600 years until God could tolerate the sin no more and brought a flood to destroy all but eight people. During the dispensation of Human Government, God granted civil authority to govern society, but once again, mankind rebelled and created the Tower of Babel. It was then through the dispensation of Promise that God created the nation of Israel from Abraham and his descendants. Then Moses received the dispensation of Law, but unfortunately, the Hebrews consistently broke the commandments. However, the Law was finally fulfilled in Christ. The Lord then established the dispensation of Grace, where God's mercy and grace would allow the believers in Jesus to have a lasting relationship with Him.

The dispensation of Grace includes both Jews and Gentiles. Mankind's responsibility during this period is to believe and have faith in Jesus while the Holy Spirit indwells believers as the Comforter (John 14:16-26). This dispensation has lasted for almost 2,000 years, and many believe it will end with the **Rapture** of all born-again believers from the earth as they go to heaven with Christ. Following the Rapture will be the **Tribulation** on Earth lasting for seven years. It will be a time of turmoil, yet the gospel of Jesus Christ will be taken to all parts of the world.

7th dispensation is called the **Millennial Kingdom of Christ** and will last 1,000 years. Prophecies to the Jewish nation will be fulfilled as *Christ returns and becomes their King*. Believers will be the only people allowed to enter the Kingdom. Satan will be bound for 1,000 years, then released for a period of time. A final conflict will occur, and God will kill all of Satan's evil armies. *The Great White Throne Judgment* will happen, and all unbelievers from the beginning of time will be judged by Jesus and then cast into the Lake of Fire (along with Satan, the Antichrist, the False Prophet, Death, and Hades) for an eternity of torment. At this point, the old world will be eliminated, and God will establish a **New Heaven and New Earth**.

The Covenants in the Bible:

A) ***Adamic Covenant*** made between God and Adam. This covenant said Adam would have everlasting life based on his obedience to God (Genesis 1:28–30).
B) ***Noahic Covenant*** made between Noah and God. In this covenant, God promised to never destroy the earth by water again (Genesis 9:11).
C) ***Abrahamic Covenant*** made between God and Abraham. God promised to make Abraham the father of a great nation and that all the world's nations would be blessed through him (Genesis 12:3; 17:5).
D) ***Mosaic Covenant*** made between God and Israel. God promised He would be faithful to Israel as a holy nation (Exodus 19:6).
E) ***Davidic Covenant*** made between David and God. God promised to have someone of David's line on his throne forever (2 Samuel 7:12–13; 16).
F) ***New Covenant*** made between Christ and the Church. This is where Christ promises us eternal life by grace through faith (1 Corinthians 11:25).
G) ***Everlasting covenant*** refers to God's eternal promises (Genesis 17:7).
*Some add the ***Eternal Order*** as an 8th dispensation.

God has divided human history into ages that may be long or short. What distinguishes them is not their length of time but the way God deals with mankind in them. While God Himself never changes, His methods do. He works in different ways at different times. Therefore, we think of a dispensation as how God deals with people during any period of history.

God and Time

"*In the beginning God...*" indicates that God was already in existence at the beginning of recorded time. Once God completed all of Creation, including the creation of time, "*God saw all that he had made, and it was very good*" (Genesis 1).
This tells us about God's eternality: "*Before the mountains were born or you brought forth the earth and the world, from everlasting to everlasting you are God*" (Psalms 90:2).

Since we measure everything in time, it is tough to conceive of something that has no beginning, has always been, and will continue forever. However, **God was and is forever**. To understand more about God and time, we need to accept the fact that the creation of the world was by the divine act of a sovereign God. We take time as a given and study its passage and measurement, but we have difficulty understanding time itself. None of us has total control over our life or time; we can only use them as God permits.

Man lives in a physical world with its four known time dimensions: length, width, height (or depth), and time. However, God dwells in a different realm—the spirit realm—beyond the perception of our physical senses. God is not limited by the physical laws and dimensions that govern our world. Since God is omniscient (knowing everything, all-knowing, all-wise, and all-seeing), He can observe all events throughout the course of our history as if they were simultaneous and can thus know what our future holds without also affecting our present, or our free will.

There continues to be profound disagreement about God's relation to time. The scholarly traditional view on God and time has been that God is timeless in the sense of being outside time altogether. Perhaps the dominant view of philosophers today is that he is **temporal**. This means He is within time, but everlasting. God has always existed and will never go out of existence, and He exists at each moment. Others believe that

God is not in our time but in His own time, and undoubtedly other views come into play. God's eternity is contrasted with man's temporality. God's perspective on time is far different from mankind's.

> ***"But do not forget this one thing, dear friends: With the Lord a day is like a thousand years, and a thousand years are like a day"*** (2 Peter 3:8).

The time that passes on earth is of no consequence from God's timeless perspective. A second is no different from a billion years; a billion years pass like seconds to the eternal God. Even though our finite minds cannot possibly comprehend this idea of the timelessness of God, we still try to relate an infinite God to our time schedule. It's an impossible task since Man operates in a lowly timeframe, while God is elevated as the *"high and exalted One who lives forever, whose name is holy"* (Isaiah 57:15).

> ***"From everlasting to everlasting You are God"*** (Psalms 90:2).

> ***"Your throne was established long ago; you are from all eternity"*** (Psalms 93:2).

So, what is time? It is simply a measured duration. Your watch indicates a change, which is the passage of time. We will never recover the minutes that have passed. Time for man began when God created the heavens and the earth. It's hard to imagine, but God exists through the course of time like other people and things; however, unlike other people and things, God has no beginning and no end. God created time, so He obviously can exist outside of it.

Defining time is a problem for most of us because it limits what we can and cannot do. In Genesis, we are told that God established the days, He gave us the sun, moon, and stars to help us measure time, and He established the week and the regularity of both work and rest. Then, in Daniel, we are told of the "time of the end" and the "end of the days" while the book of Revelation looks to when time will cease to be.

In most cases, time is much easier to accept than to define scientifically. In a worst-case scenario, time is our enemy because it leads us to death. God has revealed to us in the Bible that the world we know has a clear beginning, a continuing course, and an ending. Time for us is recorded as history, but with faith in God, we are rewarded with time being eternal.

Our time and destiny were planned:

"He has saved us and called us to a holy life—not because of anything we have done but because of his own purpose and grace. This grace was given us in Christ Jesus before the beginning of time" (2 Timothy 1:9).

"In the hope of eternal life, which God, who does not lie, promised before the beginning of time" (Titus 1:2).

"For he chose us (the elect) in him before the creation of the world to be holy and blameless in his sight" (Ephesians 1:4).

"By faith we understand that the universe was formed at God's command, so that what is seen was not made out of what was visible" (Hebrews 11:3).

In other words, the physical universe we see, hear, feel, and experience was created not from existing matter but from a source independent of the physical elements we can perceive. God created time as an additional part of His creation to accommodate the workings of His purpose in His universe.

As believers, we have a deep sense of comfort knowing that regardless of the time, God is always with us, and because of this, God can always respond to our needs and prayers. And when you discuss time, the word eternity will eventually come into play. Eternity is a term used to express infinite time or something with a beginning and no end. Boy, that is hard for our finite minds to comprehend.

"God has set eternity in their hearts" (Ecclesiastes 3:1). This means that all of us who are made in the image of God have an intuitive awareness that life does not stop at the grave.

"For since the creation of the world His invisible attributes, that is, His eternal power and divine nature, have been clearly perceived, being understood by what has been made, so that they are without excuse" (Romans 1:20).

Specifically, Paul asserts that humans can easily know at least some things about God by looking at His creation. We should look at what is visible around us in nature, what God has made, and arrive at some obvious conclusions about what we can't see. Can you imagine what kind of power it would take to create this world and everything in it? To do this incredible feat would require endless and inexhaustible power. Such power could only come from God.

Jesus stated, *"Ask, and it shall be given you; seek, and ye shall find; knock, and it shall be opened unto you. For everyone that asketh receiveth; and he that seeketh findeth; and to him that knocketh it shall be opened"* (Matthew 7:7-8).

God gives every person enough knowledge during their lifetime to seek Him. Those who respond by seeking Him will always find Him. God's Word advises us to use our time wisely because He knows that many things in life can distract us from what truly matters. Do not waste your time so that you look back with regret—you do not know what tomorrow holds!

"For I know the plans I have for you," *declares the LORD,* ***plans to prosper you and not to harm you, plans to give you hope and a future"*** (Jeremiah 29:11).

"In their hearts humans plan their course, but the LORD establishes their steps" (Proverbs 16:9).

"Remember the former things of old: for I am God, and there is none else; I am God, and there is none like me, <u>declaring the end from the beginning</u>, and from ancient times the things that are not yet done, saying, My counsel shall stand, and I will do all my pleasure" (Isaiah 46:9–10).

We have one trip through life and that is a good reason to listen to this scripture: ***"Teach us to number our days, that we may gain a heart of wisdom"*** (Psalms 90:12). The Bible says that we are a mist that appears for a little while and then vanishes (Ecclesiastes 3:1–2).

"There is a time for everything, and a season for every activity under the heavens: a time to be born and a time to die, a time to plant and a time to uproot, a time to kill and a time to heal, a time to tear down and a time to build, a time to weep and a time to laugh, a time to mourn and a time to dance, a time to scatter stones and a time to gather them, a time to embrace and a time to refrain from embracing, a time to search and a time to give up, a time to keep and a time to throw away, a time to tear and a time to mend, a time to be silent and a time to speak, a time to love and a time to hate, a time for war and a time for peace."

There will be a time when Christ returns as the absolute ruler of His creation and of mankind. Nations will gather to fight at what we call the Battle of Armageddon. God's enemies will be defeated, and ***Jesus will stand as King of Kings and Lord of Lords*** on the Mount of Olives, east of Jerusalem.

It will be a time when the Antichrist and the False Prophet will be thrown into the Lake of Fire. It will be a time when Jesus will set up His kingdom and rule for 1000 years during the Millennium, and Satan will be bound. It will be a time when, at the end of the Millennium, Satan will be released, a final battle will occur, which will be won by Christ, and then a final judgment will occur, sending Satan and all unbelievers to eternal torment in the Lake of Fire. It will be a time when the New Heavens and New Earth are created. It will be a time when the faithful will begin an eternity with our Lord, Jesus Christ. It will be a time that all Christians have been praying for.

Jesus Family and the Apostles

Much discussion has taken place regarding the life of Jesus, his parents, and his brothers and sisters. My original challenge (I didn't think it was a challenge at the time) was to identify Jesus's brothers and sisters. This turned out to be more difficult than it seemed, and part of the problem is how people were named back in Jesus' time.

Scripture states that Jesus had four brothers and at least two sisters.

> *"From whence hath this man these things? and what wisdom is this which is given unto him, that even such mighty works are wrought by his hands?* **Is not this the carpenter, the son of Mary, the brother of James, and Joses (Joseph), and of Juda, and Simon? and are not his sisters here with us?"** (Mark 6).

This earliest gospel record names the brothers rather matter-factly but does not explicitly name the sisters. So now we get into the problem area, which is related to how the people in this period were named.

In the gospel's original text, we find the Greek word "adelphos." This can mean brothers, a half-brother or stepbrother, or even other relationships like cousins or nephews. The same could be true for the word sister in Greek, "adelfí."

For example, in 1 Chronicles 23:21–22, the sons of Kish married their "sisters," a literal translation of the text, but they really married their cousins. In the older Hebrew and Aramaic languages, no special word existed for cousin, nephew, aunt, half-brother or half-sister, stepbrother or stepsister; so, they used the word brother. In the case of a cousin, the naming convention might be *"the son of the brother of my father."* As you trace many biblical characters, it sometimes becomes unclear if they are blood kin, half-brother/sister, or cousins. And keep in mind, even in our church today, we refer to folks as my *"brothers and sisters."* Jewish names were very limited back then, and Mary might have been the most common female name. The point is that not much can be made connection-wise between two mentions of the same name unless the person is identified in some other way.

So, what was Jesus' last name? It wasn't Christ, that was His title. **Christ is a Greek word meaning "anointed one."** He would have been called "***Jesus, son of Joseph***" or "***Jesus of Nazareth***." Galileans distinguished themselves from others with the same first name by adding either "son of" and their father's name, or their birthplace.

This long-standing debate about the exact relationship of the brothers to Jesus goes back to the early centuries of the Church. On the one hand, in the Catholic tradition, these have always been regarded as the cousins of Jesus. It is not stated that they were the children of Mary. Many of the Orthodox Churches hold the position that Jesus' brothers and sisters were Joseph's children from a marriage prior to that of Mary, which had left him widowed. These debates will continue.

Four views are being offered:

(1) **They were Jesus' actual siblings**—brothers/sisters, half-brothers/sisters, sons/daughters of Joseph and Mary, and therefore younger than Jesus.

(2) **They were His stepbrothers**, that is, children of Joseph by a previous marriage; and thus all older than He and not His blood relatives at all.

(3) **They were the cousins of Jesus on the mother's side**, according to some, or on Joseph's side, according to others.

(4) **That they were siblings**, but their father was not Joseph.

However, the idea that Jesus had brothers is supported by other scriptures. Paul's reference to his visit to Jerusalem states that he saw only Peter, and "*James,* **the Lord's brother**" (Galatians 1:18-19). Jesus' siblings are mentioned as accompanying Jesus and his mother to Capernaum after the marriage at Cana. This is where Jesus turned the water into wine. John tells us that during the ministry of Jesus, "even His brothers did not believe in Him" (John 7:5). Later, however, they became active leaders in the church, with two of them (James and Jude) writing letters that became part of the New Testament.

Matthew and Mark state that Jesus was the son of Mary, and the brother of James, and Joses (Joseph), and of Juda, and Simon, and He did have sisters.

<u>**So, how old was Jesus?**</u> By tracing the history recorded in the New Testament, especially the Gospel of Luke, and comparing it with Roman history, it is thought that Jesus was born between 6 and 4 BC, near the time of King Herod's death. To estimate, let's just say Jesus was born in 5 BC. John the Baptist started preaching in the fifteenth year of Tiberius's reign, when Pontius Pilate was governor of Judea, which would be AD 28 or 29. Jesus was probably baptized and began His ministry in this timeframe, 30+ years old (Luke 3:1).

Based on the number of Passover feasts Jesus observed during His public ministry, three of which are mentioned in Scripture, He ministered for approximately three and a half years. That would end Jesus' ministry and His crucifixion around AD 33. **Jesus was thought to be about 33 years old when He died.** However, some scholars heavily contested

Jesus' age and date of death. Finding one specific answer on His birth and death is difficult, depending on which calendars or accounts of Jesus' final days people use.

So, let's discuss Mary, **the mother of our Lord Jesus**. Luke 1 records Mary's conversation with the angel *Gabriel*, who told her she was to be the mother of God's Messiah. At that time, Mary was a young virgin engaged to be married to a man named Joseph. Luke 2:1-7 also confirms that Joseph and Mary, though betrothed, were considered husband and wife by Jewish customs even though the actual marriage ceremony had not been fully effectuated. Their marriage was not consummated physically until after Jesus' birth (Matthew 1:24-25).

The birth of Jesus was the result of a supernatural gift given by God to Mary and the world. God himself testified at Jesus' baptism: "This is my beloved Son!" **(Matthew 3:17).**

John 3:16 states that Jesus is God's only begotten son. When Jesus was on the cross, both the apostle John and Mary, the mother of Jesus, stood nearby.

> "When *Jesus saw his mother there, and the disciple whom he loved standing nearby, he said to her, 'Woman, here is your son,' and to the disciple, 'Here is your mother.' From that time on, this disciple took her into his home*" (John 19:26-27).

Mary was most certainly a widow and an older woman at this point in her life. Though she had other sons, Jesus chose John to care for Mary after His death. Why? Perhaps because he was recognized as the oldest son, or maybe because Jesus' brothers did not become believers until after His resurrection (John 7:5). Mary probably continued to stay with John in Jerusalem until her death.

The *Assumption of Mary* (or the Assumption of the Virgin) is the teaching that after the mother of Jesus died, she was resurrected, glorified, and taken bodily to heaven. The word assumption comes from a Latin word meaning *"to take up."* The Roman Catholic Church and, to a lesser degree, the Eastern Orthodox Church teach the Assumption of Mary.

The story of Mary's Assumption, involving her resurrection and the miraculous gathering of the apostles to witness the event, is not in the Bible. Mary is last mentioned when the Holy Spirit came upon her, and many others, on the Day of Pentecost (Acts 2:1-4).

Mary most likely lived out her remaining years in John's home. We don't know exactly where John lived, but he may have had a house in Jerusalem or Ephesus. Some have suggested that, since John probably oversaw many of the churches in Asia Minor, Mary moved to Ephesus with John and was part of the Ephesian church where Timothy pastored (1 Timothy 1:3). One tradition says that Mary died in AD 43, and another in AD 48. Still, once again, we have no way of confirming either date, but she was probably in her late 50s.

A second Mary in the Bible is **Mary Magdalene**. This Mary was a follower of Christ, and Jesus had cast seven demons from her (Luke 8:2). This deliverance would have certainly increased her dedication and love for the Lord. When Jesus arose from the dead, Mary Magdalene brought the news of the empty tomb to Peter and John, and was the first person to see the risen Christ (John 20:1, 18).

A third Mary in the Bible is **Mary of Bethany**. This Mary was the sister of Lazarus and Martha. They lived in Bethany, a town near Jerusalem. Before Jesus' arrest, Mary of Bethany anointed Jesus' head with costly oil. Jesus told those gathered in the room that Mary had done so in preparation for His burial (Matthew 26:6-13).

A fourth Mary in the Bible is identified as **Mary the mother of James the younger and Joseph and the wife of Clopas** (Luke 6:15). She is also mentioned in Mark 15:40; Matthew 27:56; and John 19:25; as watching the crucifixion of Christ. This Mary appears again in Mark 16:1 and Matthew 28:1. She is referred to as "the other Mary."

A fifth Mary in the Bible is **Mary the mother of John Mark**. She is mentioned in Acts 12:12. She had opened her home for believers to meet for prayer, and it was during one of their prayer meetings that Peter was miraculously released from prison. This Mary's son is the author of the Gospel of Mark.

A sixth **Mary** in the Bible is mentioned as a church member at Rome. Paul includes her as one of the many people to greet at the end of the Apostle's Epistle to the Romans letter. He describes her as one "who worked very hard" on behalf of the church (Romans 16:6). So now that we are familiar with all the Marys, let's look at the husband of Mary, the mother of Jesus.

Joseph is Jesus' earthly, adoptive father, but not His biological father. The suggestion that Joseph was married previously is entirely fictional, and there is no scriptural evidence that Joseph was married to anyone but Mary. Catholic tradition, along with Catholic theology, holds that Mary remained a virgin after giving birth to Jesus.

It is often tempting to try to make Scripture say something it does not say to create a theology we like. But we should remember: ***Always let Scripture interpret Scripture.*** We get into trouble when we try to make God's Word fit our preconceived ideas or a doctrine we find comforting.

Suppose other children had been present before Joseph's marriage to Mary. In that case, they would likely have been mentioned in one of the gospel accounts, especially Luke's detailed description of the trip to Bethlehem (Luke 2:1-20), and Matthew's report of the subsequent flight to Egypt (Matthew 2:13-15). The angel tells Joseph, "Get up,... take the child and his mother and escape to Egypt. Stay there until I tell you, for Herod is going to search for the child to kill him." Joseph will take two people, Mary and Jesus, not a larger brood from a previous marriage (verse 13).

Then the angel again tells Joseph, *"Get up, take the child and his mother and go to the land of Israel, for those who were trying to take the child's life are dead. So, he got up, took the child and his mother and went to the land of Israel"* (Matthew 2:20–21). Again, only Mary and the Christ Child are mentioned.

Luke tells of a time when Jesus was 12 years old and was left behind after a Passover feast at the Temple by His father and his mother. After this, Joseph seems to disappear (Luke 2:41–52).

Jesus is called *"son of Joseph"* or referred to as *"the carpenter's son"* a few times, but Joseph himself never appears in any narratives, and nothing further is related about him. The absence of Joseph in the stories of Jesus' ministry has led many to believe that Joseph died sometime between when Jesus was a young boy and when He launched His public ministry as an adult (Luke 3:23).

I want to mention another item of interest: that we need to understand the early Jewish cultural and religious context. If a man died early, according to the Torah, or Law of Moses, the oldest surviving unmarried brother was obligated to marry his deceased brother's widow and bear a child in his name so that his dead brother's "name" or lineage would not perish. This is referred to as a "Levirate marriage" or "yibbum" in Hebrew, and it is outlined in the Torah (Deuteronomy 25:5–10).

Matthew mentions that Tamar and Ruth were widows involved in Levirate marriages. In these times, this practice was normal, required, and honorable. Honoring a man who died without an heir and thus ensuring his posterity was one of the most sacred and holy things a family could do. Customs were much different back in those days. I am not suggesting that this situation occurred with Joseph, but I only mention it to clarify the traditions of that time period.

Women Present At The Crucifixion
All four gospels note that women from Galilee who followed Jesus were present at the crucifixion. However, the list showing each woman present is slightly different.

Mark lists the names of three of these women: 1. <u>Mary Magdalene</u>, 2. <u>Mary, the mother of James the younger and of</u>

Joses, and 3. Salome (Mark 15:40). Mary Magdalene was Jesus's well-known companion. Salome, mentioned only by Mark, is perhaps the mother of the two fishermen James and John, who were part of the Twelve (Luke 5:10).

Matthew, who used Mark as his source, has the same list with slight changes: 1. Mary Magdalene, 2. Mary, the mother of James and Joseph, 3. The mother of the sons of Zebedee (Matthew 27:56).

Luke drops the names and simply says that "women" were present, just as he did earlier with the names of Jesus's brothers (Luke 23:49, 55).

John list 1. Jesus' mother Mary, 2. His mother's sister, 3. Mary, the wife of Clophas, and 4. Mary Magdalene (vs.19:25). The inclusion of Mary Magdalene does not surprise us, as she is on all the lists. But John tells us explicitly that Mary, the mother of Jesus, was present.

***Salome**: There are two women named Salome in the Bible. One Salome was righteous; the other unrighteous. The righteous Salome was the wife of Zebedee (Matthew 27:56), the mother of the disciples James and John, and a female follower of Jesus. Some think she was a sister of Jesus. This Salome was the one who came to Jesus with the request that her sons sit in places of honor in the kingdom (Matthew 20:20-21). The other Salome was part of the Herod dynasty and was involved in beheading of John the Baptist (Mark 6).

The Twelve Apostles

In Judaism, dedicated apprentices followed a rabbi. Jesus of Nazareth formed a special teacher-student relationship with twelve specific men. The normal was for someone to approach a rabbi and ask to be taught by him, but Jesus did the reverse by choosing the men He called them to follow Him. Was it an accident that Jesus chose twelve? Probably not.

God's chosen people, the Israelites, were divided into twelve tribes. As Jesus calls out new people for Himself, perhaps he starts with twelve men who will form the basis of a new Israel. We find the names of the 12 disciples in (Matthew 10:2-4; Mark 3:14-19; and Luke 6:13-16).

> *"One of those days Jesus went out to a mountainside to pray, and spent the night praying to God. When morning came, he called his disciples to him and chose twelve of them, whom he also designated apostles:* **Simon** *(whom he named Peter), his brother* **Andrew**, **James**, **John**, **Philip**, **Bartholomew**, **Matthew**, **Thomas**, **James** *son of Alphaeus,* **Simon** *who was called the Zealot (designation of merit, die-hard, extremist),* **Judas** *son of James, and* **Judas Iscariot**, *who became a traitor."*

Jesus was about 30 years old when He began His public ministry (Luke 3:23), and in Jewish culture, disciples (or students) were generally younger than their teacher. Many of the disciples worked as fishermen, so they were old enough to work full-time. Peter was already married when he began following Jesus because his sick mother-in-law is mentioned (Matthew 8:14). A young man's discipleship training under a rabbi would usually start between the ages of 13 and 15.

Peter, Simon Peter, also known as **Cephas** (John 1:42), was one of the first followers of Jesus Christ. Peter, meaning rock, was originally from Bethsaida (John 1:44) and lived in Capernaum (Mark 1:29). Both cities are on the coast of the Sea of Galilee. He was married, and James and John were partners in a profitable fishing business (Luke 5:10).

Simon met Jesus through his brother Andrew, who had followed Jesus after hearing John the Baptist proclaim that Jesus was the Lamb of God (John 1:35-36). He was an outspoken and ardent disciple, one of Jesus' closest friends, an apostle, and a "pillar" of the church (Galatians 2:9).

Peter drew his sword, attacked the high priest's servant, and was immediately told to sheath his weapon. Peter boasted that he would never forsake the Lord, even if everyone else did. Later, he denied knowing the Lord three times.

However, Christ dearly loved him and held a special place among the twelve. He, James, and John formed the inner circle of Jesus' closest companions. These three alone were given the privilege of experiencing the transfiguration and a few other extraordinary revelations of Jesus. After the resurrection, Peter became a bold evangelist and missionary and one of the most outstanding leaders of the early church.

Andrew was Peter's brother and a son of Jonas. He lived in Bethsaida and Capernaum and was a fisherman on the Sea of Galilee. Andrew and Peter were called to follow Jesus at the same time (Matthew 4:18). Andrew, a simple fisherman, transformed into an extraordinary "Fisher of Men" after leaving his nets behind and following Jesus.

James the Greater was the Son of Zebedee and a member of Christ's inner circle, which included his brother, the apostle John. He and John earn a special nickname from the Lord: "*Boanerges*," which means "Sons of Thunder." When Jesus was walking by the Sea of Galilee, He called to James and John, who were "in a boat with their father Zebedee, preparing their nets" (Matthew 4:21). James and John immediately left their father to follow Jesus. The promptness of their obedience to Jesus' call may indicate that Zebedee and his sons were already familiar with Jesus' ministry and that Zebedee fully approved of his sons' calling. In those days, following a rabbi and learning from him was an honor, and it would have reflected well on Zebedee and his family.

John the Apostle, not to be confused with John the Baptist, is the author of five New Testament books: the gospel of John, the three short epistles that also bear his name (1 John; 2 John; 3 John; and the book of Revelation. John was privileged to witness Jesus' conversation with Moses and Elijah on the Mount of the Transfiguration (Matthew 17:1-9).

Probably younger than James since he is usually mentioned after him. He had a fiery temperament, a special devotion to the Savior, and had an enormous impact on the early Christian church. John raced Peter to the tomb on the first Easter morning after Mary Magdalene reported it was empty.

Although John won the race, he humbly allowed Peter to enter the tomb first (John 20:1-9). John's is the only gospel that records Jesus washing the disciples' feet (John 13:4-16). Jesus' simple act of servanthood would have impacted John greatly. This willingness to serve others and suffer for the gospel's sake must have enabled him to bear his final imprisonment on Patmos.

In the opening of the book of Revelation, which he received from the Holy Spirit during this time, he referred to himself as, *"your brother and companion in the suffering and kingdom and patient endurance that are ours in Jesus"* (Revelation 1:9). He had learned to look beyond his earthly sufferings to the heavenly glory that awaits all who patiently endure.

Philip was one of the first followers of Jesus Christ, who played a larger role in the Gospel of John than he does in the other three Gospels. Philip asks Jesus, *"Lord, show us the Father, and we will be satisfied."* Jesus replies, *"Have I been with you all this time, Philip, and yet you still don't know who I am? Anyone who has seen me has seen the Father!"*

Nathanael is believed to be the disciple **Bartholomew**. Bartholomew is a Hebrew surname meaning *"son of Tolmai."* When the apostle Philip called him to come and meet the Messiah, Nathanael was skeptical, but he followed along anyway. As Phillip introduced him to Jesus, the Lord declared, *"Here is a true Israelite, in whom there is nothing false."* Immediately, Nathanael asked, "How do you know me?" Jesus got his attention when he answered, *"I saw you while you were still under the fig tree before Philip called you."* Well, that stopped Nathanael in his tracks. Shocked and surprised, he declared, *"Rabbi, you are the Son of God; you are the King of Israel."* Nathanael was a loyal follower of Jesus.

Matthew was also called Levi. Matthew's Gospel, along with the Gospels of Luke, John, and Mark, tells an inspired and accurate history of the life of Christ. His Gospel is the longest of the four; some scholars believe it was the first to be written. Before Matthew became a disciple of Christ, he was a tax collector or "publican" in Capernaum. He taxed imports and exports based on his judgment (Matthew 9:9; 10:3). The Jews hated him because he worked for Rome and betrayed his countrymen. But when Matthew the dishonest tax collector heard two words from Jesus, "Follow me," he left everything and obeyed.

Thomas was also called "*Didymus*" (John 11:16; 20:24), the Greek equivalent of the Hebrew name Thomas, both meaning "twin." We learn from Thomas's life that he was deeply committed to his master, yet he struggled with doubts and questions. He is often referred to as "*Doubting Thomas*" because he refused to believe that Jesus had risen from the dead until he saw and touched Christ's physical wounds.
After Jesus confirmed Thomas's faith, He addressed all future readers of John's Gospel with these words:

***"Thomas, because you have seen Me, you have believed. Blessed are those who have not seen and yet have believed"* (John 20:29).**

These words reach down through the ages to help and encourage all of us who have not seen the resurrected Christ and yet believe in Him.

James the son of Alphaeus, also called **James the Less,** was one of Jesus' twelve apostles, and one of three people named James mentioned in the New Testament (Matthew 10:2–3). Some Bible versions call him "James the Younger", but the word may also imply smallness of stature or a lesser importance. Besides being listed as a disciple, little is known about James, the son of Alphaeus. He is distinguished from the other Jameses in the Bible by his father's name. The second James of the twelve apostles is described as "James the son of Zebedee" (Mark 3:17). The third James mentioned was the brother of Jesus (Galatians 1:19), a leader in the Jerusalem church (Acts 12:17; Galatians 2:9), and the author of the Book book of James).

Simon the Zealot has little in the Bible told about him. He is mentioned in the Gospels in three places, but only to list his name. In Acts 1:13, we learn that he was present with the apostles in Jerusalem's upper room after Christ ascended to heaven.

Judas (Jude) – Thaddaeus – Son of James is another of the least known disciples. Jude is a derivative of the names Judas and Judah, much as the nickname Sam is a derivative of Samuel. Judas the apostle is identified in the gospels as *"not Iscariot."* So, Jesus chose two men named Jude (or Judas) to be among the twelve disciples (John 14:22; Acts 1:13).

Another Jude was the son of Mary and Joseph and would have been raised as a brother to Jesus Christ (Mark 6:3). This Jude was not one of the twelve apostles but was the author of the New Testament book by that name. Jude was among the siblings of Jesus who initially did not believe His claims to be the Messiah (John 7:3–5). They lived in the same household with the Son of God for years, yet they did not believe in Him. **They knew about Him, but they did not know Him. The same is true for many professing Christians today.

Judas Iscariot was the treasurer for the group and used this trusted position to steal from their resources (John 12:6). Iscariot refers to Kerioth, a region or town in Judea, and another idea is that it relates to the Sicarii, a cadre of assassins among the Jewish rebels. Money was important to Judas. As already mentioned, he was a thief, and, according to (Matthew 26:13–15), the chief priests paid him "thirty silver coins" to betray the Lord. Jesus knew from the very beginning what Judas Iscariot would do. Jesus told His disciples, **"Have I not chosen you, the Twelve? Yet one of you is a devil!"** (John 6:70).

At the Last Supper, Jesus predicted His betrayal and identified the betrayer: "Jesus answered, *'It is the one to whom I will give this piece of bread when I have dipped it in the dish.' Then, dipping the piece of bread, he gave it to Judas Iscariot, son of Simon"* (John 13:26). Jesus said that Judas Iscariot was not "clean", had not been born again, and was not forgiven of his sins (John 13:10–11). Judas was empowered to do what he did by the devil himself: *"As soon as Judas took the bread that Jesus had given him, Satan entered into him"* (John 13:27).

Judas Iscariot betrayed the Lord with a kiss, but after committing his atrocious act, Judas was seized with remorse and threw the thirty silver coins into the temple. The Bible presents two accounts of Judas Iscariot's death: Matthew says he hanged himself after returning the silver, while Acts describes him buying a field with the money, falling headlong, and his body bursting open. The death of Judas Iscariot was a suicide committed after he was filled with remorse (but not repentance) for his betrayal of Jesus.

Concerning how Judas died, here is a simple reconciliation from Matthew 27:5 about the issue: Judas hanged himself in the potter's field, and that is how he died. Then, after his body had begun to decay and bloat, the rope broke, or the branch of the tree he was using broke, and his body fell, bursting open on the land of the potter's field (Acts 1:18–19).

Concerning who paid for the field, here are two possible ways to reconcile the facts:

1) Judas was promised thirty pieces of silver several days before Jesus' arrest (Mark 14:11). During the days leading up to his betrayal of Jesus, Judas made arrangements to purchase a field. However, no money had yet been transferred. After the deed was done, Judas was paid, but he then returned the money to the chief priests. The priests, who considered the silver "blood money," completed the transaction that Judas had begun and bought the field.

2) When Judas threw the thirty pieces of silver down, the priests took the money and used it to buy the potter's field (Matthew 27:7). Judas may not have purchased the field personally, but he provided the money for the transaction and could then be said to be the purchaser.

The people called that field in their language "*Akeldama*," that is, "Field of Blood." *Jesus said, "The Son of Man will go just as it is written about him. But woe to that man*

who betrays the Son of Man! It would be better for him if he had not been born" **(Matthew 26:24).**

The Apostles' Deaths
Here are the most popular "traditions" concerning the deaths of the apostles:

Peter was passionate until the end. Historians record that when Peter was sentenced to death by crucifixion, he requested that his head be turned toward the ground because he did not feel worthy to die in the same manner as his Savior (John 21:18).

Andrew was crucified on an X-shaped cross in Greece. After seven soldiers whipped Andrew severely, they tied his body to the cross with cords to prolong his agony. When he was led toward the cross, his followers reported that Andrew saluted it in these words: *"I have long desired and expected this happy hour. The cross has been consecrated by the body of Christ hanging on it."* He continued to preach to his tormentors for two days until he died.

According to the New Testament, **James the Great** was the second apostle to die after Judas Iscariot, and the first to be martyred. Herod the King, usually identified with Herod Agrippa, had James executed by the sword.

John faced martyrdom when the Roman emperor Domitian commanded that he be thrown into a boiling pot of oil, but he was miraculously delivered from death. John was sentenced to slave labor in the mines of Patmos, where he wrote his prophetic book of Revelation. Tradition says that John was later freed, possibly due to old age, and he returned to what is now known as Turkey. He died as an old man sometime after AD 98, the only apostle to die peacefully.

Philip preached the gospel in Phrygia, in Asia Minor, and is thought to have died a martyr there at Hierapolis.

Bartholomew, known as Nathanael, was a missionary in Armenia, Phrygia, and Hierapolis with Philip. He witnessed in present-day Turkey and was martyred for his preaching in Armenia, being flayed to death by a whip.

Matthew suffered martyrdom in Ethiopia, killed by a sword wound in Alexandria.

Thomas – Stabbed with a spear in India during one of his missionary trips to establish the church there.

James the Less – Son of Alphaeus was one of the three James mentioned in the New Testament. Thought to have taken the gospel to Persia (modern Iran) and was stoned to death there.

Simon the Zealot is mentioned four times in the New Testament, and tradition says that he preached the gospel in Persia and was ultimately killed for refusing to give a sacrifice to the sun god.

Judas (Jude) Son of James (not Iscariot), suffered martyrdom in Beirut, in the Roman province of Syria. He and the apostle Simon the Zealot were usually connected. The axe that he is often shown holding in pictures symbolizes how he was killed.

Judas Iscariot was filled with remorse after betraying the Lord with a kiss and threw the thirty silver coins into the temple. Then he went away and hung himself.

***Additional information:**

James the brother of Jesus, was the church leader in Jerusalem. He was thrown from the southeast pinnacle of the temple (over a hundred feet down) when he refused to deny his faith in Christ. When they discovered that he survived the fall, his enemies beat James to death with a club. This is thought to be the same pinnacle where Satan had taken Jesus during the temptation.

Matthias the apostle chosen to replace the traitor Judas Iscariot, was stoned and then beheaded.

Apostle Paul seemed to be anticipating his soon-to-be demise: *"For I am already being poured out as a drink offering, and the time of my departure has come. I have fought the good fight, I have finished the race, I have kept the faith.* Henceforth there is laid up for me the crown of righteousness, which the

Lord, the righteous judge, will award to me on that Day, and not only to me but also to all who have loved his appearing" (2 Tim. 4:6–8). Eusebius, an early church historian, claimed that the order of the Roman emperor Nero beheaded Paul. The martyrdom occurred shortly after much of Rome burned in a fire—an event that Nero blamed on the Christians. Paul was beheaded and not crucified because Roman citizens were usually exempt from crucifixion. Based on what the Book of Acts records of Paul's life, we can assume he died declaring the gospel of Christ and spending his last breath as a witness to the truth that sets men free (John 8:32).

Stephen was one of the first seven deacons chosen by the early Christian community and became an evangelist. His success in converting Jews drew the ire of the Sanhedrin (the supreme rabbinic court), and his punishment for speaking against "this holy place and the law" was to be stoned to death.

Herod imprisoned **John the Baptist** because he reproved Herod for divorcing his wife (Phasaelis) and unlawfully taking Herodias, the wife of his brother Herod Philip I. Herodias' daughter, whom Josephus identifies as Salome, danced before the king and his guests on Herod's birthday. Her dancing pleased Herod so much that, in his drunkenness, he promised to give her anything she desired, up to half of his kingdom. When Salome asked her mother what she should request, she was told to ask for the head of John the Baptist on a platter. Although Herod was appalled by the request, he reluctantly agreed and had John executed by beheading him in the prison. In art, the episode is known as *"The Feast of Herod."*

So, what have we learned from these deaths? It is not so important how the apostles died, but it is very important that they were all willing to die for their faith. If Jesus had not been resurrected, the disciples would have known it. People will not die for something they know to be a lie. The fact that all the apostles were willing to die horrible deaths, refusing to renounce their faith in Jesus, is tremendous evidence that they had truly witnessed the resurrection of Jesus Christ.

Who Owns The Land?

Just a brief background to refresh our minds about the land Jehovah promised to Israel.

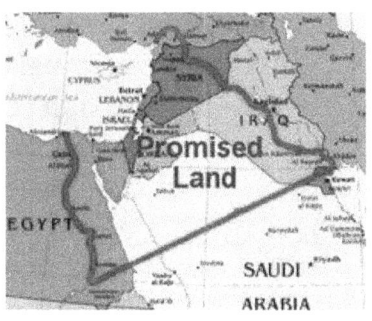

"To your descendants I give this land, from the river of Egypt to the great river, the Euphrates" (Genesis 15:18).

God later confirmed this promise to Abraham's son, Isaac, and Isaac's son, Jacob (whose name was later changed to Israel). This was repeated: *"Your territory will extend from the desert to Lebanon, and from the great river, the Euphrates—all the Hittite country—to the Great Sea on the west"* (Joshua 1:4).

Translated today, **Jehovah gave Abraham and his descendants all the land modern Israel currently possesses, all the land of the Palestinians, all the land of Jordan, and some of Egypt, Syria, Iraq, and Saudi Arabia.** It is referred to as the "**Promised Land**" because it was the territory God had promised to Abram, later renamed Abraham. The territory was included in what is called the **Abrahamic Covenant**, and it is described in Genesis 12:1-4.

In the covenant, God promised Abram that he would become a great nation, have a land of his own, and bless those who blessed him and curse those who cursed him. The Bible prophesied that even though much conflict would occur, the Promised Land would be given to the Jewish people again sometime after the second coming of Jesus (Ezekiel 47:13-20). Scripture shows that God has a dispute with those involved in *"dividing up My land"* (Joel 3).

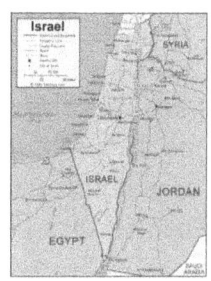 ***Israel*** is the world's only Jewish state and is bounded to the north by Lebanon, to the northeast by Syria, east and southeast by Jordan, southwest by Egypt, and west by the Mediterranean Sea. The geography of Israel is very diverse, with desert conditions in the south and snow-capped mountains in the north. Israel's area is approximately 8,019 square miles, which includes 172 square miles of inland water. Israel stretches 263 miles from north to south, and its width ranges from 71 miles at its widest point to 6.2 miles at its narrowest point.

As of 2023, approximately 7.2 million Jewish people lived in Israel, about 73% of the country's total population. This makes Israel the world's largest Jewish population center, with over 46% of the world's Jewish population living there. God chose the nation of Israel as the place where ***Jesus Christ*** would be born—the Savior from sin and death (John 3:16). God confirmed that the Messiah would come from the line of Abraham, Isaac, and Jacob.

> *"For you are a people holy to the Lord your God. The Lord your God has chosen you to be a people for his treasured possession, out of all the peoples who are on the face of the earth. It was not because you were more in number than any other people that the Lord set his love on you and chose you, for you were the fewest of all peoples"* (Deuteronomy 7:6-7).

Beginning in the 8th century BC, Jews in Israel were repeatedly conquered and deported from their homelands for centuries by foreign empires. These exiles involved Assyria, Babylonia, Persia, Greece, and Rome. Israel was then divided into two kingdoms: Israel in the north and Judah in the south. Many people were captured and forcibly moved, while others fled elsewhere to escape wars or the risk of being sold into slavery. As a result, Jews eventually spread all over the world, bringing their customs and religion with them. Thus, the diaspora (scattering) caused the spread of Judaism worldwide.

Another group in this area is the **Palestinians**. These are an Arab ethno-nationalist group residing primarily in the West Bank, the Gaza Strip, Israel, Jordan, and parts of southern Lebanon and Syria. Significant Palestinian communities are in other countries as well, including Saudi Arabia and the United States, which is home to about 85,000 people of Palestinian descent. There are roughly 14.5 million Palestinians in the world, and nearly 98% of all Palestinians are Muslim. Over 5 million live in the West Bank and the Gaza Strip, and another 2 million in Israel. In ancient times, Palestine was part of the region of Canaan, which was made up of the Kingdoms of Judah and Israel. Palestinians (Arab Muslims) want to establish a state by that name on all or part of Israel.

The Israeli-Palestinian conflict is about who gets what land and how it's controlled. Although both Jews and Arab Muslims date their claims to the land back a couple of thousand years, the current political conflict began in the early 20th century. Jews fleeing persecution in Europe wanted to establish a national homeland in what was then an Arab-Muslim majority territory in the Ottoman and later British Empire. The Arabs resisted, seeing the land as rightfully theirs. An early United Nations plan to give each group part of the land failed, and Israel and the surrounding Arab nations fought several wars over the territory.

Today's lines largely reflect the outcomes of two wars, one waged in **1948** and another in **1967**. In 1947, the United Nations adopted Resolution 181, the *Partition Plan*, which sought to divide the British Mandate of Palestine into Arab and Jewish states. On **May 14, 1948, the State of Israel was created**, sparking the first Arab-Israeli War. After the creation of Israel in 1948, Egypt controlled Gaza for nearly two decades.

Israel's victory in the ***1967 Six-Day War*** against its Arab neighbors allowed it to control the Gaza Strip and the West Bank, and for the next 38 years, it controlled the Strip and enabled the construction of 21 Jewish settlements. Since 1967, **Jerusalem** has been wholly under the rule of the State of Israel. Long an object of conflict, the holy city of Jerusalem has been governed, both as a provincial town and a national capital.

After the Six-Day War of 1967, **Bethlehem** was part of the Israeli-occupied territory of the West Bank. In 1995, Israel ceded control of Bethlehem to the newly established **Palestinian Authority** (PA) in preparation for a two-state solution. Today, the West Bank, home to a large Palestinian population, is nominally controlled by the *Palestinian Authority* and is under Israeli occupation. Israeli troops enforce Israeli security restrictions on Palestinian movement and activities, and Israeli "settlers" (Jews) build ever-expanding communities in the West Bank that effectively deny the land to Palestinians and Hamas.

Hamas is an Islamist militant group that spun off from the Palestinian branch of the *Muslim Brotherhood* in the late 1980s. It took over the Gaza Strip after defeating its rival political party, **Fatah**, in elections in 2006. Governments, including the United States and European Union, have designated Hamas a terrorist organization over its attacks against Israel, which have included suicide bombings and rocket attacks. Israel declared war on Hamas following its surprise assault on the country in October 2023.

Hezbollah is a Shiite Muslim political party and militant group based in Lebanon, where it has fostered a reputation as "a state within a state." Founded during the chaos of the fifteen-year Lebanese Civil War (1975-1990), the Iran-backed group is driven by its violent opposition to Israel and its resistance to Western influence in the Middle East. It functions as a proxy of Iran, its largest benefactor. Israel's killing of Hezbollah leader Hassan Nasrallah in September 2024 has dealt the militant group a severe blow. Yemen's Houthis are a Zaydi Shiite movement that has been fighting Yemen's Sunni majority government since 2004.

The **Houthis** took over the Yemeni capital, Sanaa, in September 2014 and seized control over much of northern

Yemen by 2016. Yemeni officials and Sunni states have repeatedly alleged that Iran and its proxy Hezbollah have provided arms, training, and financial support to the Houthis. Iran is widely accused of backing the Houthis.

Iran – Since the Iranian Revolution in 1979, the government of the Islamic Republic of Iran has faced accusations from several countries regarding its training, financing, and provision of weapons and safe havens for non-state militant actors, including Hezbollah, Hamas, and other Palestinian groups such as the Islamic Jihad (IJ) and the Popular Front for the Liberation of Palestine (PFLP).

These groups are designated terrorist groups by several countries and international bodies such as the EU, UN, and NATO, but Iran considers such groups to be "national liberation movements" with a right to self-defense against Israeli military occupation. Iran uses these proxies across the Middle East and Europe to create instability, expand the scope of the Islamic Revolution, and carry out terrorist attacks against Western targets in the regions. As Iran becomes more powerful, it becomes more of a problem for Israel and the United States.

Russia is quietly strengthening its partnerships with Iran-aligned militia groups throughout the Middle East. While Russia's military alliance with Hezbollah in Syria is well-documented, its relationships with Iran militias are often overlooked. Russia engages with **Hashd al-Shaabi** in Iraq, defends Hezbollah from terrorism allegations, and negotiates with the Houthis. These relationships bolster the Russia–Iran partnership and will seemingly strengthen in the future.

Any decision that could influence a change in Israel involves many issues. Who would control the Jerusalem municipal boundaries? Would any part of Judea and Samaria be included in the Palestinian state? Who would control the Mount of Olives and the Western Wall? Could an agreeable solution be made for the control of the Temple Mount?

Some believe these and other issues could be solved by establishing Palestine as an independent state in Gaza and most of the West Bank, leaving the rest of the land to Israel. It sounds good, but has much opposition. Perhaps you develop a "one-state solution," wherein all the land becomes either one big Israel, one big Palestine, or some shared state with a new name. It's hard to imagine this happening.

A reminder: God owns all this land and gave it to Israel.

So here are some of today's news headlines:

Hezbollah (Lebanese) is fighting Israel to support its Palestinian ally Hamas.

Iran backs Palestinian groups such as Hamas.

Israel recently killed the Hezbollah leader.

Iran hates Israel and the USA.

Israel recently launched airstrikes against Iran (near Tehran).

Nine countries support Palestine: Argentina, Brazil, China, India, Indonesia, Russia, Saudi Arabia, Turkey, and Spain.

Ten countries right now do not support Palestine unless direct negotiations between Israel and the PA occur: Australia, Canada, France, Germany, Italy, Japan, Mexico, South Korea, the UK, and the USA.

Israel, the USA, and Qatar recently announced negotiations for a ceasefire and hostage release in Gaza (Not sure if Hamas will participate).

Israel airstrikes bomb Hezbollah and Hamas.

North Korea sends troops to support Russia in the fight against Ukraine.

Quick Look at Possible Future Events:

The national election is over, and Donald J. Trump has been elected President of the United States for a second time. Trump has become only the second president in U.S. history to win two nonconsecutive terms, following in the footsteps of

Grover Cleveland. Trump knows all the major political figures around the world, so let's assume that he can negotiate a peaceful solution to the conflicts in the Middle East involving Israel. And if this happens, perhaps peace will continue for a long time in the future.

Israel is finally at peace, so now let's look at (Ezekiel 38:11):

> *"I will go up against a land of unwalled villages; I will go to a peaceful people, who dwell safely, all of them dwelling without walls, and having neither bars nor gates."*

Gog will be the leader of a great army that attacks the land of Israel, which is *"peaceful and unsuspecting"* at the time. Could the battle described by Ezekiel be closer than we think? The Bible mentions some nations that attack Israel.

The Battle of Gog/Magog (Ezekiel 38, 39), is led by the leader Gog, the prince of Rosh, Meshech, and Tubal—possibly a chief of the Scythians, a savage and cruel nomadic people. Magog is the name of a land, country, or territory—possibly the southern part of Turkey, Syria, Iran, Iraq, Russia, Europe, and China. Most think it is Russia. Some believe that *Gog/Magog* is just a term representing evil forces opposed to God.

A coalition of nations invades Israel – (Persia (Iran), Ethiopia (Sudan), Put (Libya), possibly Algeria and Tunisia, Gomer and Beth-Togarmah (Turkey). Others believe the coalition is composed of parts of Europe, Russia, Iran, Iraq, Syria, Turkey, Armenia, Libya, countries south of Egypt, and China.

Many Islamic forces are involved. Gog and his massive army will cover the land of Israel like a cloud. God will supernaturally destroy Gog and his army by using fire, brimstone, and hail. God showcases His power and sanctity to all the nations.

Perhaps at this time, to possibly prevent future wars, <u>Israel signs a Peace Agreement</u> with the head of the 10-Nation European Confederation. The head of this confederation will be the ***Antichrist***. (**Clock starts on the 7-Year Tribulation**). The sequence of things that may occur is:

The Rapture
Judgment Seat of Christ for Believers (The Bema)
Marriage Supper of the Lamb
Tribulation Begins: Lasts for 7 years
Two Witnesses: prophesy on earth for 3 ½ years
144,000 Israelis: begin evangelism on earth
An angel will preach the gospel to every nation
The Temple in Jerusalem is rebuilt
Antichrist breaks peace covenant after 3 ½ years
Abomination of Desolation
Great Tribulation Begins: lasts 3 ½ years
False Prophet dictates worship of the Antichrist
Mark of the Beast (666) is required for all
Second Coming of Jesus Christ and His Army
Battle of Armageddon
Antichrist and False Prophet into the Lake of Fire
Satan is chained and sent to the Abyss for 1000 years
Babylon is destroyed
Tribulation Ends
Beginning of the Millennium
End of the 1000-year Millennium: Satan is released
Satan and a massive world army attack Jerusalem
God destroys the army with fire from heaven
Satan now joins the Antichrist and False Prophet in the Lake of Fire (Hell)
Great White Throne Judgment
Jesus hands the Kingdom over to God the Father
New Heavens and New Earth are Created
God lives with His people on the New Earth for Eternity

Credits

(Sources used to develop these documents)

The Bible (primarily the KJV)

Billy Graham literature

Dr. David Jeremiah literature

Pastor Mark Wilke

Scholar Gary Ray

GotQuestions

Unsealed.org

Wikipedia

Tim LaHaye and Thomas Ice

Phoenix Seminary

Baptist Standard

BibleStudyTools.com

Theology and Ministry

Basic internet searches

Randy Alcorn

Gene Nethery

Joe Johnston

www.ingramcontent.com/pod-product-compliance
Lightning Source LLC
Chambersburg PA
CBHW070551050426
42450CB00011B/2818